STG Devotional Series

Justin Jenkins

Table of Contents

Introduction

To My Fellow Readers

I. Why STG?

When I was about six years old, I had a moment that changed the trajectory of my life. It was either a dream or a figment of my imagination. Nevertheless, I was alone in an open space. From what I recall, the space was entirely pitch black or dark blood red. While I was in the open space, I heard a deep thunderous voice. It proclaimed, "Obey God. Resist the devil!"

I'm not sure whether the voice was from God, from His angels, or was in my head, but I was certain of two facts. One fact was that the voice scared the wits out of me. The following morning, I ran to my mother, hugged one of her legs, and told her what happened. It was at that moment that I became a Christian. I believed on the Lord Jesus Christ for my salvation and trusted Him to save me from utter destruction.

The other fact is that what the voice said to me can be found in Scripture. James 4:7 says, *Submit to God. Resist the devil and he will flee from you*. I believe the Lord used James 4:7 to draw me to Him. Remember that *faith comes by hearing, and hearing by the word of God* (Romans 10:17). When the gospel and the Holy Scriptures are heard, people can be convicted to repentance. Therefore, I decided to name my book "STG Devotional Series" after James 4:7 (Submit to God).

II. How STG *Devotional Series* Began

I started to write *STG Devotional Series* in 2019. I was at a group called Faith RXD Morris County, where the first half of the meeting involves a physical workout, and the second half involves a spiritual workout that includes a devotional time. I became one of the leaders there and was asked to share a devotional with the group. I noticed that the other leaders got their content online from an established pastor or ministry. However, I wanted to do something different and create my own content, so I wrote a devotional based upon Ephesians 5:16, and I shared it with the group.

I wrote a few more devotionals during the following months, and by the end of the year, an idea had popped into my head. I could gather all the devotionals that I wrote and make a collection out of them. However, I needed help. I didn't know how many devotionals to write or what Bible verses to choose, so I asked my family members, friends, and acquaintances what their favorite Bible verses were. Some people shared their favorite verses with me without me even having to ask.

III. The Purpose of *STG Devotional Series*

STG Devotional Series consists of fifty-two devotionals and is based on the favorite Bible verses of my family members, friends, and acquaintances. I picked the number fifty-two so that a devotional could be done every week throughout the entire year. The purpose of this book is to accurately teach the Scriptures from the Bible verses selected. This way, you can get a better understanding of the verses, their context, and what the authors were trying to convey to their audiences.

Another purpose of this book, which is more important, is to share the good news of the gospel. Ask yourself the following questions: If today was your final day on earth, where would you be going after you died, and why? If there is an afterlife and you had to spend eternity either in heaven or in hell, where would you be? If there is only one way to heaven, how would you make it there?

All of these questions can be answered through the gospel of Jesus Christ. *It is appointed for men to die once, but after this the judgment* (Hebrews 9:27). Unless Jesus returns to the earth first, you'll eventually die. Whether it's today, tomorrow, or many years later, everyone has an expiration date. After your death, you'll stand before the Almighty God and give an account for your life. You will have to testify for every deed you've done, and even for every word you have spoken.

At the judgment, you will encounter at least two issues. One is that your good works aren't good enough to get you into heaven. *All our righteousnesses are like filthy rags* (Isaiah 64:6). The second issue is sin. *Sin is lawlessness* (1 John 3:4). It is rebellion against God and His laws. As Ray Comfort of Living Waters ministry explains, if you have lied, stolen, yelled out "Jesus Christ" in frustration, lusted after someone, put anything ahead of God, or violated any other part of God's law, then you stand guilty before Him. Even if you only break one commandment in your entire life, you're still guilty. *Whoever shall keep the whole law, and yet stumble in one point, he is guilty of all* (James 2:10). You don't get charged for the good things you do, but for the crimes you've committed. Likewise, God doesn't determine your fate based upon the good you've done, but upon all the sins in your life.

If you die in your sins, there are grave consequences. First, you will go to hell, which can be compared in a way to jail. It will not be a place of partying, but of anguish and torment in extreme heat. Then you will be transported to the Great White Throne Judgment, which is akin to the courtroom. At the judgment, God will convict you as a guilty sinner and violator of His law. Next, He will send forth His angels, who are like the security guards, to take hold of you and cast you into the lake of fire. This is the eternal prison, where you will burn for eternity. There will be no purgatory or any form of parole to bail you out. That is found nowhere in Scripture.

The good news in all of this is that God doesn't want you or anybody else to suffer such a horrific fate. Hell was only meant for the devil and his angels. God provided a way out for us. He sent His Son, Jesus Christ, to die as punishment for our sins. Although He was without sin, He demonstrated His love and laid down His life for us all (Romans 5:8). Because of His crucifixion, death, burial, and resurrection, you don't have to suffer in hell.

Instead, you can have a relationship with God, as well as the gift of eternal life. If you have yet to do so, *repent, and believe in the gospel* (Mark 1:15). "Repent" is *metanoeó* in Greek (Strong's 3340), which means to change your mind. You turn away from a lifestyle of sin. You go from loving sin to hating it. Therefore, *if we confess our sins, He is faithful and just to forgive us our sins and to cleanse us from all unrighteousness* (1 John 1:9). If you repent of your sins, God will forgive you.

Believe on the Lord Jesus Christ for your salvation. He is God in the flesh. He died to pay the price for your sins, and He is the only one who can save you from eternal destruction. *I am the way, the truth, and the life. No one comes to the Father except through Me* (John 14:6). You don't get to have a relationship with God or enter into heaven unless it's through Jesus Christ alone. Therefore, *believe on the Lord Jesus Christ, and you will be saved* (Acts 16:31).

IV. Conclusion

My prayer is that through *STG Devotional Series*, you may get a better understanding of the Word of God, as well as of the gospel of Jesus Christ. My other prayer is that if you have yet to believe on the Lord Jesus for your salvation, that you will do so as soon as possible. *Now is the accepted time; behold, now is the day of salvation* (2 Corinthians 6:2). May the good Lord bless you throughout this entire reading, as well as in your personal life.

Godspeed,
Justin Jenkins

Lesson 1

No Temptation Has Overtaken

To My Brother in Christ, Johnny C.

No temptation has overtaken you except such as is common to man; but God is faithful, who will not allow you to be tempted beyond what you are able, but with the temptation will also make the way of escape, that you may be able to bear it.

—1 Corinthians 10:13

I. Introduction

Have you ever felt led to do something, even if it isn't good for you? Perhaps you found a wallet. You see a lot of money in it and now feel inclined to take some for yourself. Maybe you had a rough week at work. To blow off some steam, you consider drinking to the point where you get drunk and black out. Perchance you're on the internet. While you're on the web, you feel enticed to look at explicit content on an adult website. Maybe someone cut you off on the highway, and you get the urge to go after the person and tell them off.

The scenarios listed above are examples of temptation. A temptation can be defined as an enticement to do something, even if it isn't good for you. Either an outside influence or an inner impulse has attracted your attention. As a result, you feel led to take something into consideration. In your mind, you know that the activity may not be good for you. However, there is instant pleasure and gratification

5

in the activity. Therefore, you convince yourself that the pros outweigh the cons, which makes it more difficult not to give in.

II. Context

In 1 Corinthians 10:13, the apostle Paul spoke to the Christians at Corinth about temptation and the power it can have over someone: *No temptation has overtaken you except such as is common to man.* Paul then spoke about God's power over temptation: *But God is faithful, who will not allow you to be tempted beyond what you are able, but with the temptation will also make the way of escape, that you may be able to bear it.*

III. Main Points

As Paul told the church at Corinth, *No temptation has overtaken you except as is common to man.* If you have had the urge to do something, especially an activity that may be sinful or that may not be good for you, know that you aren't alone. *There is nothing new under the sun* (Ecclesiastes 1:9). Temptations are a part of life. Hence, it *is common to man.* It has been around since the beginning of time, and everyone has experienced it at some point.

Because everyone has experienced temptation, it is likely that others have gone through the same ones as you. If people have faced the same temptation as you, it is likely that some of those people did not give in to that temptation. Therefore, if there are people who have overcome the same temptations that you face, there's hope. There's hope in that you don't have to be overtaken by temptation. The fact that others have endured and overcome them can give you motivation to do the same.

Also, *God is faithful, who will not allow you to be tempted beyond what you are able.* The main reason that you can endure temptation is because God is faithful. "Faithful" in Greek is *pistos*, which means trustworthy (Strong's 4103). God is trustworthy because He has your best interests in mind. He does not want you to succumb to temptation. He knows how much you can be tempted before you give in to it. Hence, He'll limit the intensity of the enticements that head your way. He will not let Satan or any other influence push you beyond your breaking point. He will not make you feel as if giving in is your only option.

God *will also make the way of escape, that you may be able to bear it.* Not only does God put restrictions on how much you'll be tempted, but He will also provide a way out for you. He can provide you with the strength to endure enticements and walk away from them. The Lord gives you strength through His Word. *Your word I have hidden in my heart, that I might not sin against You* (Psalm 119:11). The Lord can also give you strength through godly people. Godly people can help keep you accountable, as well as inspire you to live in righteousness. *He who walks with wise men will be wise* (Proverbs 13:20).

IV. Conclusion

At some point, each of us has been overtaken by a temptation that *is common to man.* This temptation is the enticement to sin. It's common to man because everyone has given in to the temptation to sin. *But God is faithful.* Although we may have sinned against God and His commandments, we can still trust Him. The reason is that He *will not allow you to be tempted beyond what you are able.* He will not allow the temptation to sin to be so strong that we're automatically doomed.

He made *the way of escape* through His Son, Jesus Christ. Jesus escaped temptation in the wilderness, and He escaped the temptation to sin throughout His entire life. Because of this, He could be the perfect sacrifice for the punishment of the sins of the whole world. Because of Jesus, we don't have to be overtaken by the temptation to sin. We can escape the everlasting consequences of sin, which is eternal death in hell and, eventually, the lake of fire. Instead, we will be able to bear the temptation to sin through Him. So if you have yet to do so, *believe on the Lord Jesus Christ, and you will be saved* (Acts 16:31).

V. Discussion Questions

1. What are your initial thoughts? Is there anything that stuck out to you while reading this?

2. Define temptation. What are some temptations that are *common to man*?

3. In what ways can temptation overtake someone?

4. What are some ways you can combat temptation?

5. If God promises to *make the way of escape* for temptation, how can it increase your appreciation for Him?

6. Can you recall a time when you overcame temptation? If so, how did you overcome it?

7. Is there anything that you can take away from this discussion and apply to your life? Any final thoughts?

Lesson 2

Meditate on These Things

To My Brother in Christ, German G.

Finally brethren, whatever things are true, whatever things are noble, whatever things are just, whatever things are pure, whatever things are lovely, whatever things are of good report, if there is any virtue and if there is anything praiseworthy—meditate on these things.

—Philippians 4:8

I. Introduction

Think of a time when you set your focus on something. For instance, maybe you had your mind on the assignments you had to do at work, or you thought about how you want to spend quality time with your family and friends. Maybe you contemplated a new diet and workout regime that would get you in better shape. Perhaps you pondered how to introduce yourself to the person you're interested in.

These are cases of meditation. To meditate means to deeply think about something. You have gained enough interest in someone or something that it has gotten your attention. Because it has gotten your attention, you begin to set your focus on it. The more you increase your focus on something, the more you will think about it.

II. Context

In Philippians 4:8, the apostle Paul gave an exhortation in regard to meditation. He told the church at Philippi what they should meditate on: *Finally, brethren,*

9

whatever things are true, whatever things are noble, whatever things are just, whatever things are pure, whatever things are lovely, whatever things are of good report, if there is any virtue and if there is anything praiseworthy—meditate on these things.

III. Main Points

So what should you meditate on? *Whatever things are true.* When something is true, it's in alignment with reality. It matches with the events that have taken place. You should focus on whatever is true because the truth will guide you in the right direction. With the truth, you can make assessments of the situations you encounter and proceed with sound decisions. The ultimate source of truth is the Word of God, which is inerrant. It is 100 percent correct, without any error. Hence, His *word is truth* (John 17:17). In order to meditate on whatever things are true, set your focus on God and His Word.

Whatever things are noble. "Noble" is defined as having or showing admirable qualities. If you can focus on that which is noble, then you can strive to possess admirable qualities in yourself. The more noble qualities you have, the more you can reflect godly character. So if you meditate on that which is noble, you're more likely to *add to your faith virtue, to virtue knowledge, to knowledge self-control, to self-control perseverance, to perseverance godliness, to godliness brotherly kindness, and to brotherly kindness love* (2 Peter 1:5–7).

Whatever things are just. "Just" is translated in Greek as *dikaios*, which means innocent, holy, and righteous (Strong's 1342). God's way is perfect, which means He is the standard of innocence, holiness, and righteousness. You should set your mind on that which is just in order to know what is right and holy in the sight of God. The Lord calls us to be holy because He is holy (1 Peter 1:16). Therefore, the more you dwell on that which is just, the more you may think to become set apart, as well as to become a reflection of His holiness.

Whatever things are pure. "Pure" is defined as clean or free from any contamination. When you mediate on what is pure, you can cleanse your mind from any filth. *Every word of God is pure* (Proverbs 30:5). So when you set your mind on God and His Word, it's as if you have spiritual soap. With it, you're able to scrub off the dirt that stems from uncleanness and lewdness.

Whatever things are lovely. "Lovely" is *prosphiles* in Greek, which means pleasing and acceptable (Strong's 4375). When you focus on what is pleasing and acceptable to the Lord, you can think about how you can be obedient to Him. Obedience is a way you can worship the Lord and show your love for Him. Remember—if you love Him, keep His commandments (John 14:15). Therefore, if you think on that which is lovely, you're more likely to be obedient to Him and fulfill the great commandment, which is to love *the Lord your God with all your heart, with all your soul, and with all your mind* (Matthew 22:37).

Whatever things are of good report. A good report can have a positive influence on you. Whenever you think about a story that has a desired outcome or a testimony that exhibits admirable behavior, it may uplift your spirit. You can be happy for others, as well as praise God for the good report. Think about it—you are to *rejoice with those who rejoice* (Romans 12:15). A good report can also motivate you. Seeing someone succeed may inspire you to follow suit and do better as well.

If there is any virtue. "Virtue" is translated in Greek as *arête*, which means excellence and valor (Strong's 703). When you meditate on things that have virtue, you're more likely to think about moral excellence. You program your mind to *abhor what is evil*, as well as to *cling to what is good* (Romans 12:9). In this way, you can look to do what is right according to the Lord, as well as flee from all forms of wickedness.

When you meditate on whatever has virtue, you're also likely to concentrate on things that have valor. "Valor" is defined as bravery and boldness in the face of adversity. You don't crumble under pressure, but you remain steadfast and stoic. Boldness is an important quality to have since it can be difficult to stand up for what is right, especially when it may result in negative consequences. Remember: *the righteous are bold as a lion* (Proverbs 28:1).

If there is anything praiseworthy. If something is categorized as praiseworthy, then it's worthy of approval and admiration. When you think on that which is praiseworthy, you can consistently give thanks to the Lord. You should thank Him because He created the universe and gave you life. He is worthy *to receive glory and honor and power; for [He] created all things* (Revelation 4:11). You should also thank Him whenever something good happens since He is the reason it occurs. *Every good gift and every perfect gift is from above, and comes down from the Father of lights* (James 1:17).

IV. Conclusion

Meditate on the gospel of Jesus Christ. What is true is that Jesus took on human flesh and dwelled on the earth. What's noble is the amazing and admirable example He set forth in His life. What's just is that Jesus was innocent of any wrongdoing.

Throughout His thirty-three years on earth, He lived a sinless life. What's pure is Jesus's intentions throughout His ministry. He *did not come to call the righteous, but sinners, to repentance* (Mark 2:17). What's lovely is that He laid down His life for all of mankind. His sacrificial act was acceptable and pleasing to His Father in heaven.

The gospel has a good report because it has been preached throughout most of the world. It has spread throughout Jerusalem, all Judea, Samaria, and the uttermost parts of the earth (Acts 1:8). The gospel has also been talked about for more than two thousand years. The gospel has virtue since Jesus upheld moral excellence in the face of adversity. He upheld godly character even when people falsely accused Him, spat on Him, and mocked Him while He was on the cross. The gospel is praiseworthy because it reminds us to be thankful for God loving us enough to sacrifice His Son for our sins. So if you have yet to meditate on the gospel, do so today! *Now is the accepted time; behold, now is the day of salvation* (2 Corinthians 6:2).

V. Discussion Questions

1. What are your initial thoughts? Is there anything that stuck out to you while reading this?

2. When you think of meditation, what comes to mind? Why?

3. Out of the different attributes Paul mentioned (true, noble, just, pure, lovely, good report, virtue, and praiseworthy), which ones do you meditate on the most? Why?

4. Out of the different attributes Paul mentioned (true, noble, just, pure, lovely, good report, virtue, and praiseworthy), which ones should you meditate on more? Why?

5. How can meditating on the attributes Paul mentioned help you in your walk with the Lord?

6. Think of a time when you or someone else meditated on the attributes Paul mentioned. What was the result?

7. Is there anything that you can take away from this discussion and apply to your life? Any final thoughts?

Lesson 3

A Heart of Flesh

To My Brother in Christ, Ryan S.

Then I will give them one heart, and I will put a new spirit within them, and take the stony heart out of their flesh, and give them a heart of flesh.

—Ezekiel 11:19

I. Introduction

Have you ever removed anything that was old and put something new in its place? For instance, the tires on your car are worn down to the point that there's no tread on them. Hence, you decided that it was time to get a new set of wheels. Perhaps one of the light bulbs in your house burned out, so you removed it and put a new light bulb in its place. Maybe the mouse for your computer stopped working because the battery died. As a result, you took the dead battery out of the mouse and inserted a new one.

If your answer is yes, then you have replaced something. To replace means to take something away and put another entity in its place. Replacement usually happens when an object is outdated, worn down, or no longer functioning. It no longer gives you the results you desire. Therefore, you replace it with a new commodity, based upon the belief that it will provide the intended result.

II. Context

In Ezekiel 11:19–20, the prophet Ezekiel gave a prophecy of the Lord in regard to replacement. He stated that the Lord would change Israel's spiritual condition. He prophesied that the Lord would remove their hardened hearts toward Him and provide them with a new heart, as well as a new spirit: *Then I will give them one heart, and I will put a new spirit within them, and take the stony heart out of their flesh.* Ezekiel then talked about how Israel's new heart and spirit would result in a change of lifestyle: *that they may walk in My statutes and keep My judgments and do them.* Ezekiel additionally mentioned that Israel's new spiritual condition would affect their relationship with the Lord: *and they shall be My people, and I will be their God.*

III. Main Points

Just as the Lord promised the people of Israel a new heart and a new spirit, so He will do the same for you—as long as you put your trust in Him. He will give you one heart, and He will put a new spirit within you. "Heart" is *leb* in Hebrew, which means the feelings, will, or center of anything (Strong's 3820). "Spirit" is the word *ruach* in Hebrew, which refers to the mind and life (Strong's 7307).

If the Lord gives you one heart, He provides you with the feelings to love Him, the will to be in alignment with His desires, and Himself to be at the center of your life. When He gives you a new spirit, He puts the mind of Christ in you so you can think in the same manner as the Lord Jesus Christ. He also gives you spiritual life with the Holy Spirit. Think about it: *He who raised Christ from the dead will also give life to your mortal bodies through His Spirit who dwells in you* (Romans 8:11).

He will take the stony heart out of your flesh and give you a heart of flesh. Stones are recognized as hard, solid mineral matter of which rock is made. So a stony heart can be a representation of sinful desires because you can be *hardened through the deceitfulness of sin* (Hebrews 3:13). "Stony" is *eben* in Hebrew, which means "carbuncle" (Strong's 68). A carbuncle is a group of pus-filled bumps that form a connected area of infection under the skin. Therefore, a stony heart can also symbolize feelings and desires that are infected by sin.

"Flesh" is *basar* in Hebrew, which means skin or body (Strong's 1320). The skin and human body are much softer than a stone. So if something stony represents something that is hardened and closed off, it's safe to assume that "flesh" can represent something that is softer and more open. Thus, in this context, the heart symbolizes feelings and desires to hear the words of the Lord and do them.

When the Lord takes the stony heart out of your flesh, He removes the hardened attitude that doesn't want to submit to God. He also takes away the infected mindset that is corrupted by wickedness. When He gives you the heart of flesh, it signifies that He replaced your sinful nature with the desire to serve Him. *Therefore, if anyone is in Christ, he is a new creation; old things have passed away; behold, all things become new* (2 Corinthians 5:17). If you put your trust in the Lord, old things, such as the stony heart, are no longer part of you. Behold, all things, such as the heart of flesh, are new in you.

The Lord gives you a heart of flesh that you may walk in His statutes and keep His judgments and do them (Ezekiel 11:19–20). More often than not, an inner change of wants and desires will result in a difference of outward actions. So if the Lord gives you the desire to serve Him through the heart of flesh and His Spirit, you're more likely to be obedient to His Word and precepts.

You shall be His, and He will be your God. When the Lord gives you a new Spirit and heart, it signifies change from a nonexistent relationship to that of kinship. The Holy Spirit is the seal that shows you are a son or daughter of the Most High God. It's the promise that you're His and that one day He will redeem you. You will get to be with Him, reign with Him, and live with Him forever.

IV. Conclusion

The Lord Jesus Christ is *gentle and lowly in heart* (Matthew 11:29). Although He was God in the flesh, He was gentle and humble in character. He lowered Himself and laid down His life for the sins of the whole world. Through Christ's death, burial, and resurrection, He can give you one heart and will put a new spirit within you. The Holy Spirit is accessible to anyone who believes on Him.

If you have yet to do so, repent of your sins and believe on the Lord Jesus Christ. He will take the stony heart out of your flesh, and give you a heart of flesh. He will give you the heart to follow Him. In this way, you may walk in His statutes and keep His judgments and do them. Also, you shall be a part of His people, and He will be your God (Ezekiel 11:19–20). You can have an everlasting relationship with Him, and one day, you can be with Him forever.

V. Discussion Questions

1. What are your initial thoughts? Is there anything that stuck out to you while reading this?

2. When the Lord stated, *I will give them one heart, and I will put a new spirit within them*, what does this indicate? What does this tell you about the Lord?

3. Why is it necessary for the Lord to remove the stony heart out of our flesh?

4. What are the differences between the *stony heart* and the *heart of flesh?*

5. How can a change of inner motives and desires result in a difference of outward actions?

6. In what ways does the promise *They shall be My people, and I will be their God* give you an appreciation for the Lord?

7. Is there anything that you can take away from this discussion and apply to your life? Any final thoughts?

Lesson 4

Live Peaceably with All

To My Sister in Christ, Emily M.

If it is possible, as much as depends on you, live peaceably with all men.

—Romans 12:18

I. Introduction

Think about all the people you interact with. How well do you get along with them? How are the relationships in your family? Do you and your friends enjoy each other's company? Can you work with your coworkers as a team? Are you at least civil with your neighbors? How do you treat strangers or people of a lower socio-economic class?

Based upon how you interact with others, you can get an estimate on your level of affability. "Affability" is defined as the quality of having a friendly and good-natured manner. If you're an affable person, you have a peaceful demeanor in which people are more comfortable around you. People find it easier to approach you and talk to you. As a result, your chances of pleasant interactions and good relationships increase.

II. Context

In Romans 12:18, the apostle Paul gave an exhortation in relation to affability. He told the Roman Christians how they should follow his exhortation: *If it is possible, as much as depends on you.* Paul then mentioned the exhortation: *live peaceably*. He additionally informed them who they should live peaceably with: *with all men.*

III. Main Points

As Paul urged the church at Rome to do, you are to *live peaceably* as well. To live peaceably means to act in a manner that is calm and not contentious. When you live peaceably, you seek to be in harmony with those around you. Whenever an issue arises, you search to find solutions to the problem. You don't try to start strife, dissension, or drama, but you look to put a peaceful end to them.

You are to *live peaceably* because if you do so, you can be a reflection of the Lord and His character. You are to be *imitators of God as dear children* (Ephesians 5:1). Children are known to be more impressionable since adults tend to be set in their ways. So like impressionable children, you're to imitate the Lord and live peaceably since peace is a part of His character. One of the names of God is Jehovah Shalom: the Lord is my peace. Peace is also one of the nine parts of the *fruit of the Spirit*, the godly attributes of the Holy Spirit (Galatians 5:22–23).

You are to *live peaceably* because your lifestyle can serve as a witness to others. *Let your light so shine before men, that they may see your good works and glorify your Father in heaven* (Matthew 5:16). When you live a godly lifestyle, it speaks as a testimony to others. People can see that there's something different about you. And if you share your faith with them, they can at least see that you're authentic in what you believe. Not only do you talk the talk, but you also walk the walk. Therefore, by what you say and do, you may lead others to Christ.

You are to *live peaceably with all men. All men* applies to the people you get along with, but it also applies to the people you don't get along with. Is there someone in your life whom you can't stand or who rubs you the wrong way? Yes, you're to live peaceably with that person too. *If you love those who love you, what credit is that to you? For even sinners love those who love them* (Luke 6:32). One indicator of spiritual maturity is that you're able to be civil with those you don't see eye to eye with. It's easy to be non-contentious with those who are friendly, but it's harder to do so with those who are difficult to be around.

If it is possible, as much as depends on you, live peaceably with all men. You should seek to be in harmony with the people in your life, as well as with strangers, as much as you can. You should do so, even if it means you have to set aside some differences with another individual or repair a relationship. If you do so, the Lord

19

considers you blessed. *Blessed are the peacemakers, for they shall be called sons of God* (Matthew 5:9). You're considered fortunate and well-off when you try to make peace with others. It's a sign of genuine faith and is an indication that you're a child of the Most High God.

Sometimes it may not be possible to *live peaceably with all men*. One example is when someone has severe anger issues and your personal safety is in jeopardy. *Make no friendship with an angry man, and with a furious man do not go, lest you learn his ways and set a snare for your soul* (Proverbs 22:24–25). Another example is when you are with talebearers who tear others down with their backbiting and cause division with their malicious speech. *He who goes about as a talebearer reveals secrets; therefore do not associate with one who flatters with his lips* (Proverbs 20:19).

A third case is if a person is a spiritual liability. Your relationship with God comes first. If anyone tries to get in the way of your relationship with God, then that's a major concern. So if you confronted them about their sin and they refuse to repent or want you to sin with them, it may be best to part ways until they repent. *What fellowship has righteousness with lawlessness?* (2 Corinthians 6:14). But outside of such circumstances, you should try your best to be in harmony with others.

IV. Conclusion

God wants us to *live peaceably with all men*. The problem is that our iniquities have separated us from our God (Isaiah 59:2). However, God is *not willing that any should perish but that all should come to repentance* (2 Peter 3:9). So He sent His Son, Jesus Christ, the Prince of Peace, to die on the cross for all of mankind. Because of this, anyone who repents and believes in the gospel can live peaceably with God (Mark 1:15).

With Jesus, there can be reconciliation with others, as well as a restoration of relationship between God and the one who believes in Him. Through a harmonious relationship with Jesus, we can follow His Word and live peaceably with all people. He can give us His peace so we can be in harmony with the people He made. So through Christ alone, *if it is possible, as much as depends on you, live peaceably with all men.*

V. Discussion Questions

1. What are your initial thoughts? Is there anything that stuck out to you while reading this?

2. When you hear *live peaceably*, what comes to mind? Why?

3. In what ways does living peaceably with all men help you with your testimony to others?

4. How can living peaceably with difficult people help you grow in your faith?

5. Can you recall a time when living peaceably with others helped your testimony or growth in faith?

6. What are some ways you can live peaceably with others as much as possible?

7. Is there anything that you can take away from this discussion and apply to your life? Any final thoughts?

The Testing of Your Faith

To My Brother in Christ, Omar S.

Knowing that the testing of your faith produces patience.

—James 1:3

I. Introduction

Think of an action that leads to another process. For instance, you plant seeds in fertile ground. Within a few weeks, the seeds start to germinate and you can see the plants rise through the soil. Maybe you start to lift weights at the gym. After a few months of consistent exercise, your physique changes and you have more muscle mass and less fat. Perhaps you saw a person whom you were interested in and decided to talk to. The initial conversation led to a connection, then friendship, relationship, engagement, marriage, and now a family.

The examples listed above are cases of causation. Causation is the influence that one event has on another. In order for causation to take place, an action has to occur. Once the action has happened, then a reaction can come about. Hence, there is a relationship of cause and effect between the two events. The original cause is a jump start for the secondary and tertiary effects.

II. Context

In James 1:2–4, the half brother of Jesus told his Jewish brethren about the importance of trials and tribulations: *My brethren, count it all joy when you fall into various trials.* He then told them why trials are significant. In his reasoning, he included the causation of trials: *the testing of your faith produces patience.* James then gave an exhortation, which included the causation of patience: *But let patience have its perfect work, that you may be perfect and complete, lacking nothing.*

III. Main Points

So *my brethren, count it all joy when you fall into various trials.* The word for "joy" is *chara* in Greek, which means delight (Strong's 5479). So when you fall into hardship, consider it a delight. Although trials are no easy thing to go through, our outlook on them can have a big effect on how we deal with them. You can see the glass as half empty, where it's all doom and gloom, or you can see it as half full, where you use it as an opportunity to delight yourself in the Lord and grow closer to Him.

"When" is an indicator that you will encounter a trial. Notice how James wrote "when" and not "if." We can expect to face hardship at some point in our lives. *Beloved, do not think it strange concerning the fiery trial which is to try you, as though some strange thing happened to you* (1 Peter 4:12). Don't believe that it's strange when you go through difficulties, because trials are a part of life, and everyone experiences them at some point.

Know that *the testing of your faith produces patience* (James 1:3). Testing is a period when one's ability is examined. So the testing of your faith is a time when you find out how much you really trust the Lord. Patience is the ability to endure and wait for something. So when your faith is tested through trials and difficulties, you can learn to wait on the Lord and His provision, as well as trust in Him while you endure them.

But let patience have its perfect work, that you may be perfect and complete, lacking nothing (James 1:4). The perfect work in patience is that it can help shape you into a godly person. Think about it: perseverance produces character (Romans 5:4). Patience can help you grow in character so *that you may be perfect and complete.* You can be a mature person of faith. Therefore, you will lack nothing since you will have all the components needed to be steadfast in the faith.

There are a myriad of ways that patience can have its perfect work. Patience can perfect you in faith. When you wait on the Lord, you may realize that He can get you through seasons of difficulty. Patience can perfect you in longsuffering. The more you rely on the Lord, the more you can endure hardship. Patience can perfect you in hope. There's anticipation in the fact that the Lord will provide and that there is light at the end of the tunnel. The season of difficulty will eventually come to an end. Since patience can perfect you in faith, longsuffering, and hope, it can also perfect you in love. Remember that *love suffers long and is kind; . . . it believes all things* and *hopes all things* (1 Corinthians 13:4, 7).

IV. Conclusion

Our most important trial is life here on earth. We're in a fallen creation where we are prone to sin and live in defiance against God. But the consequences of sin are disastrous. It first leads to an earthly death. *The wages of sin is death* (Romans 6:23). It leads next to an eternal death—everlasting torment in hell and, eventually, the lake of fire.

The joy in the trial is that we can grow close to God through Jesus Christ. Because of Jesus's death, burial, and resurrection, we can have saving faith through Him. We don't have to go to hell. Also through Jesus, we can have growing faith since the testing of our faith produces patience. Therefore, *let patience have its perfect work, that you may be perfect and complete, lacking nothing* (James 1:4). Let the gospel of Jesus Christ transform you from the time you believe to the moment you see Him face to face in heaven. *Whoever believes in Him should not perish but have everlasting life* (John 3:16).

V. Discussion Questions

1. What are your initial thoughts? Is there anything that stuck out to you while reading this?

2. Why may it be difficult to *count it all joy when you fall into various trials?*

3. What does *when you fall into various trials* indicate? Why is this important to know?

4. How does the testing of your faith produce patience?

5. In what ways can patience help you become perfect and complete, lacking nothing?

6. Can you recall a time when a trial has helped you grow in patience and faith?

7. Is there anything that you can take away from this discussion and apply to your life? Any final thoughts?

Greater Love

To My Brother in Christ, Parker T.

***Greater love has no one than this,
than to lay down one's life for his friends.***

—John 15:13

I. Introduction

Have you ever had to give something up to help those around you? For example, maybe you were about to finish a race, but you saw that the runner ahead of you was on wobbly legs. Although you could have passed him, you decided to help him walk to the finish line. Perhaps there was only one seat left on the bus. Even though you got there first, you saw a pregnant lady standing up—so you gave up your seat so she could sit down. Maybe you saw a homeless person shivering in the cold, so you gave him clothing and food.

If you answered yes, then you have demonstrated an act of altruism. Altruism is when you sacrifice yourself for the benefit of others. You assess a situation and conclude that someone is in a less than favorable position, so you decide to help the person get to a more favorable position, even if it comes at your expense or inconvenience. You do it with no strings attached and expect nothing in return.

II. Context

In John 15:13, the Lord Jesus Christ talked to His disciples about an altruistic type of love. He told them that this type of love is superior and that no other type of love can surpass it. He also gave them an example of what altruistic love is: *Greater love has no one than this, than to lay down one's life for his friends.*

III. Main Points

As the Lord Jesus told His disciples, *greater love has no one than this, than to lay down one's life for his friends.* Love is known as a strong affection toward something. It's a choice and action where you show how much you care about a particular thing. *Love suffers long and is kind; love does not envy; love does not parade itself, is not puffed up; does not behave rudely, does not seek its own, is not provoked, thinks no evil; does not rejoice in iniquity, but rejoices in the truth; bears all things, believes all things, hopes all things, endures all things* (1 Corinthians 13:4–7).

Greater love has no one than this implies that there is a superior form of love. The Greek coins it as *agape* love (Strong's 26). Agape love fulfills the biblical definition of love and showcases it on a deeper level as compared to the other types. It shows such a high degree of love that no one can find or demonstrate a greater example of it. Hence, agape love is known as the greater love.

What is agape love? It is *to lay down one's life for his friends.* "To lay down" means to voluntarily give up. You surrender something that you treasure and possess. It can also mean to give of yourself. You sacrifice your time, resources, and finances. So to lay down your life for your friends is to place yourself in a position of selflessness. You put others before yourself.

Not only do you put others before yourself, but you do so out of pure intentions. You want to help other people so they can be in a better position than where they're currently at. So *let nothing be done through selfish ambition or conceit, but in lowliness of mind let each esteem others better than himself* (Philippians 2:3).

There is no greater love than agape love because it represents who God is. *God is love* (1 John 4:8). Also, there is nothing in the universe or heavens that is greater than the Almighty God. So if there's nothing greater than the Almighty God and He is synonymous with the definition of agape love, then what other form of love can match it? What other form of love can be parallel to or supersede agape love?

IV. Conclusion

Greater love has no man than this: Jesus's sacrificial death on the cross. The Lord Jesus laid down His life for all of mankind. Not only does this mean that the Lord Jesus laid down His life for His friends, but He did so for His enemies as well. Think about how difficult it would be to die for those who hate you, let alone anyone in general. *Scarcely for a righteous man will one die; yet perhaps for a good man someone would even dare to die* (Romans 5:7).

The Lord Jesus Christ laid down His life for all of us so that we may live. He didn't lay down His life for ulterior motives or to get something out of it. He truly did it for the good of everybody. Through Jesus, we can be free from hell and the second death. Through Jesus, we can have a relationship with God. Through Jesus, we can have the gift of everlasting life. So *believe on the Lord Jesus Christ, and you will be saved* (Acts 16:31).

V. Discussion Questions

1. What are your initial thoughts? Is there anything that stuck out to you while reading this?

2. When you think of altruism, greater love, or agape love, what comes to mind?

3. How can motives play a factor in agape love?

4. In what ways can you demonstrate agape love?

5. Why can it be difficult to demonstrate agape love?

6. What does agape love teach you in regard to God and His character?

7. Is there anything that you can take away from this discussion and apply to your life? Any final thoughts?

To Those Who Love God

To My Sister in Christ, Krystine T.

**And we know that all things work together
for good to those who love God, to those
who are the called according to His purpose.**

Romans 8:28

I. Introduction

Have you ever been in a tough situation that turned out well in the long run? For instance, maybe you grew up in a tough environment, whether it was a broken home, with abusive parents, or in a high-crime neighborhood. It may have been tough to grow up in these conditions, but you got through it. Now you're able to help those who face similar difficulties. Perhaps something you had high hopes for didn't work out, whether it was a job or a romantic relationship. Because you invested a lot into it, you were devastated. But eventually, you found something better, such as a new job or relationship—and you couldn't be any happier.

These are instances of when a situation works out. When something works out, it means that it develops in a way that's satisfactory. There is a progression of some sort that yielded positive and desirable results. The situation may not have stemmed from ideal conditions, but at the end of the day, something good came from it.

II. Context

In Romans 8:28, the apostle Paul continued his message of encouragement to the Christians in Rome. He continued to make his case in regard to how the current sufferings they've gone through will not be comparable to the future glory they will experience, as well as how the Holy Spirit will help them in their weaknesses. Therefore, he reminded the Romans Christians of an optimistic truth: *And we know that all things work together for good to those who love God.* Paul additionally stated who this optimistic truth applied to: *To those who are the called according to His purpose.*

III. Main Points

Just as Paul reminded the Roman Christians, let us remember that *all things work together for good.* "All things" means every situation, even the most difficult ones. This includes current sufferings and our weaknesses. "Work together for good" implies that there's a reason why something took place. It indicated that something was allowed for a purpose.

When it comes to our current sufferings, there's a reason why we experience hardship. There's a rationale in regard to why we have weaknesses and infirmities. So if you're in a tough spot or in a season of tribulation, know that your sufferings are not in vain. *To everything there is a season, a time for every purpose under heaven* (Ecclesiastes 3:1).

As difficult as sufferings can be, they can be used for something beneficial. For instance, your persecutions and tribulations can be used to strengthen your faith. Remember that *tribulation produces perseverance; and perseverance, character; and character, hope* (Romans 5:3–4). Your troubles can also help out other people. You're a witness to those around you, whether they are fellow Christians, family, friends, or peers. If they see that you can respond well in hardship, they may be encouraged, as well as drawn closer to Christ. Therefore, *let your light so shine before men, that they may see your good works and glorify your Father in heaven* (Matthew 5:16).

Know that all things work together for good to those who love God. "Those who love God" are those who have received God's love. They have received God's love through the Holy Spirit and have put their hope in Him. *Now hope does not disappoint, because the love of God has been poured out in our hearts by the Holy Spirit who was given to us* (Romans 5:5). Because they have received God's love, they are able to love Him in return. *We love Him because He first loved us* (1 John 4:19).

Those who love God are those who have a relationship with God. If you're in Christ, you have an inseparable connection with God and His love. *For I am persuaded that neither death nor life, nor angels nor principalities nor powers, nor things present nor things to come, nor height nor depth, nor any other created thing, shall be able to separate us from the love of God which is in Christ Jesus our Lord* (Romans 8:38–39).

Those who love God are those who are called according to His purpose. "Called" is *kletos* in Greek, which means "invited and appointed," specifically a saint (Strong's 2822). So *the called* are those who are invited, as well as appointed by God to be saints and believers. This process of invitation and appointment is according to His purpose. It's based on His intention to deliver mankind from their sufferings, groaning, and weaknesses.

IV. Conclusion

And we know that all things work together for good to those who love God, to those who are the called according to His purpose: this is demonstrated in the gospel. *For the Scripture says, "Whoever believes on Him will not be put to shame"* (Romans 10:11). One reason all things will work together for good to those love God is because He sent His Son, Jesus Christ, to save people from their sins and to provide a path of reconciliation to the Father. *For God did not send His Son into the world to condemn the world, but that the world through Him might be saved* (John 3:17).

If you have yet to do so, love God today. Love God through obedience to His commandments. Jesus said, *If you love Me, keep My commandments* (John 14:15). Therefore, obey His gospel, as well as His commandment to repent. If you love God and obey the gospel, all things will work together for good, especially in the eternal aspect. *Eye has not seen, nor ear heard, nor have entered into the heart of man the things which God has prepared for those who love Him* (1 Corinthians 2:9).

V. Discussion Questions

1. What stood out to you about the devotion and the passages discussed?

2. How do *all things work together for good to those who love God?*

3. If *all things work together for good to those who love God,* how can this truth increase your appreciation for Him?

4. What are some examples in Scripture and from personal life where *all things work together for good to those who love God?*

5. How can one love God? How can one be "the called" *according to His purpose?*

6. If *all things work together for good to those who love God, to those who are the called according to His purpose,* how can this give us a better understanding of God's purpose?

7. Is there anything that you can take away from this discussion and apply to your life?

From Whence Comes My Help?

To My Beloved Mother

I will lift up my eyes to the hills—from whence comes my help?

—Psalm 121:1

I. Introduction

Have you ever been in an unfavorable position and sought out someone's assistance? Perhaps your car broke down on the highway, so you contacted your auto insurance company for emergency roadside assistance. Maybe your house caught on fire and you dialed 911 to get the fire department to extinguish the fire. Maybe you became severely ill, so you went to the doctor's office so the doctor could determine what was wrong.

The examples above are instances when someone has looked for help. Help is known as assistance. You make it easier for someone to do something through your services and abilities. If you look to someone for help, it's because you believe he or she can assist you in your time of need. You're confident that they can get you out of a difficult position.

II. Context

The author of Psalm 121 is an example of someone who looked for help. Psalm 121 is part of the Songs of Ascents—a collection of music the Israelites sang while they traveled to Jerusalem for specific feasts. Since Jerusalem is in a mountainous region, the Israelites traveled uphill to get there. That is why the psalmist made the opening statement, *I will lift up my eyes to the hills.* Hills can represent obstacles literally and figuratively. This may be why he asked for the whereabouts of his help. *From whence comes my help?* However, the psalmist knew who the source of his help was. *My help comes from the Lord* (Psalm 121:2). Throughout the rest of the psalm, the author explained why his help came from the Lord.[1]

III. Main Points

As the psalmist did, look to the Lord for help because He *made heaven and earth* (Psalm 121:2). The Lord is the creator of the entire universe. Because He is the creator of the entire universe, He has more knowledge about how it operates than anyone else. Just as engineers have superior knowledge about the machines they built, so God has infinite knowledge about the world He built. Since the Lord made the world, He also has dominion over it. *You are worthy, O Lord, to receive glory and honor and power; for You created all things* (Revelation 4:11). What better source of help is there than the Lord, who is the omniscient creator and the ruler of all things?

He will not allow your foot to be moved (Psalm 121:3). The Lord can help you remain steadfast since He is unwavering in nature. He has told us, *I am the Lord, I do not change* (Malachi 3:6). Therefore, if you put your trust in Him, He will provide you with spiritual stability. Just as it is difficult to uproot a tree that is planted in the ground, so it is hard to pluck up a Christian who is grounded in the truth of God's Word. *He shall be like a tree planted by the rivers of water, that brings forth its fruit in its season* (Psalm 1:3).

He who keeps you will not slumber (Psalm 121:3). "Keeps" is *shamar* in Hebrew, which means to hedge, guard, and protect (Strong's 8104). In order to protect something, you need to be awake. That way you can know what's going on and can be aware of any threats that arise. The Lord is awake at all times. He is omnipotent and is conscious of what's going on. *The eyes of the Lord are in every place, keeping watch on the evil and the good* (Proverbs 15:3). Because the eyes of the Lord are in every place, He also keeps watch over the nations. *Behold, He who keeps Israel shall neither slumber nor sleep* (Psalm 121:4).

---

1   Nate Holdridge, "From Where Does Our Help Come (Psalm 121)," November 29, 2020, https://www.nateholdridge.com/blog/from-where-does-our-help-come-psalm-121.

The Lord is your keeper; the Lord is your shade at your right hand (Psalm 121:5). The Lord is the only one who can protect you at all times. *The sun shall not strike you by day, nor the moon by night* (Psalm 121:6). He has the ability to protect you at any time because He is omnipotent. That means that He is all powerful and can do anything He pleases. *Whatever the Lord pleases He does, in heaven and in earth, in the seas and in all deep places* (Psalm 135:6). Also keep note that one of His names is Jehovah Magen: the Lord is My Protector and Defender. Protection is a part of His character.

Although there are forms of earthly protection that are visible and tangible, they are not comparable to the protection that comes from the Lord. They may provide a temporary defense, but it's not impeccable. It is fallible and will eventually fail. The only reason man-made protection can work is because the Lord allows it to. *Unless the Lord guards the city, the watchman stays awake in vain* (Psalm 127:1). Unless the Lord keeps watch over you, all other forms of protection will fail.

The Lord shall preserve you from all evil (Psalm 121:7). The Lord can help you get through anything that Satan and his demons may throw your way. This includes temptations and difficult seasons in your life. So while it's a guarantee that trouble and hardship will come at some point, the Lord will not allow them to overcome you—as long as you put your trust in Him. If you're a Christian, the Lord has given you the gift of the Holy Spirit to help you in tribulation. *The Helper, the Holy Spirit, whom the Father will send in My name, He will teach you all things, and bring to your remembrance all things that I said to you* (John 14:26). The Holy Spirit can instruct you and remind you what the Lord Jesus said to you in His Word.

He shall preserve your soul (Psalm 121:7). "Soul" is *nephesh* in Hebrew, which means "life" (Strong's 8104). The Lord can prolong your days since He is the only one who gives life. He alone can also grant you eternal life—and if you believe in Him, you can receive that very gift. Although you are appointed to die once in your earthly body, you don't have to experience the second death in the glorified body. Therefore, *the Lord shall preserve your going out and your coming in from this time forth, and even forevermore* (Psalm 121:8). If you believe in Him, He shall preserve your days for eternity.

IV. Conclusion

The Lord Jesus Christ provided help in countless ways throughout His ministry. He gave the blind their sight. He cleansed the lepers of their diseases. He healed the sick of their illnesses. He helped the lame walk. He gave the deaf the ability to hear. He resurrected the dead back to life. He preached the gospel to those who were lost.

In regard to salvation, Jesus helped us by sacrificing His life to pay for our sins. If we believe on Him for salvation, His death, burial, and resurrection will help us escape the fiery pit of hell. If we repent of our sins, He will forgive us. *If we confess our sins, He is faithful and just to forgive us our sins and to cleanse us from all unrighteousness* (1 John 1:9). Therefore, if you have not yet done so, repent and believe on the Lord Jesus Christ. If you believe on Him, He can help you *from this time forth, and even forevermore*. He can help you live forever through the gift of everlasting life.

V. Discussion Questions

1. What stood out to you about the devotional and the passages discussed?

2. What are some reasons you look to the Lord for help?

3. What are some ways you can remind yourself that your help comes from the Lord?

4. Do you find it difficult to seek the Lord for help? Why or why not? If so, what are some ways you can combat that?

5. How does looking to the Lord help you in your walk with Him?

6. How has the Lord helped you in your life?

7. Is there anything that you can take away from this discussion and apply to your life? Any final thoughts?

Lesson 9

But When You Are Old

To My Brother in Christ, Lucas C.

Most assuredly, I say to you, when you were younger,
you girded yourself and walked where you wished;
but when you are old, you will stretch out your hands,
and another will gird you and carry you
where you do not wish.

—John 21:18

I. Introduction

Has there been a time in your life when you have messed up, but received another opportunity? For example, maybe you were thirty minutes late to your first date. Even though you were late, your date still wanted to meet up again. Perhaps you made an error at work and it cost your company money. Although the error was a fireable offense, your boss let you off with a warning. Maybe you failed the test for your driver's license, but you were allowed to retake it two weeks later.

These are what you call second chances. A second chance is an additional opportunity to partake in an action. It's usually given after the original opportunity was missed or blown. Whether it was due to your actions or an unfortunate set of circumstances, the initial result was that things didn't work out. However, as one opportunity is lost, another one may arise.

II. Context

In John 21:18, the Lord Jesus talked to Peter about how He will give him a second chance, despite his betrayal. Jesus reminded Peter about his first opportunity and how he conducted himself: *Most assuredly, I say to you, when you were younger, you girded yourself and walked where you wished.* Jesus then told Peter about his second opportunity. He signified that Peter would die and glorify God later in his life: *but when you are old, you will stretch out your hands, and another will gird you and carry you where you do not wish.*

III. Main Points

Just as it was with Peter, it is possible that *when you were younger, you girded yourself and walked where you wished.* "Girded" in Greek is *zónnumi*, which means to bind about, especially with a belt (Strong's 2224). The ancient Israelites girded up their garments before battle or strenuous labor. They picked up the bottom part of their tunics and tucked it into a belt so it wouldn't get in the way. Just as the Israelites girded their tunics to be ready for battle or labor, so girding yourself is to prepare yourself to engage in an activity.

Walked where you wished hints at hedonism. Hedonism is the philosophical thought that you should do whatever pleases you. *Walked where you wished* aligns with hedonism because your actions are based upon your desires. Your pleasures have enough of an influence on you that they can control how you conduct yourself.

So if *you girded yourself and walked where you wished*, you have prepared to do what you want to do. The issue with this is that what you want to do may be in contradiction with what God wants you to do. If you place your desires above God's, that is selfish ambition and idolatry. It's all about you and not about God. You're more likely to behave in such a manner when you are younger. A possible reason is that younger people tend to be less mature than those who are older. Even now, you can fall prey and do as you wish if you're not careful.

It's possible that *when you are old, you will stretch out your hands, and another will gird you and carry you where you do not wish.* To stretch out your hands can signify surrendering. When your hands are away from your body, you are more susceptible to attacks. Hence, you have given up the ability to defend yourself. For instance, law enforcement tells you to put your hands up. If you do so, it shows them that you have given up.

If *another will gird you and carry you where you do not wish,* that can show submission. If you're girded, someone has bound you in chains or handcuffs. Your movement is restricted and you can no longer do as you please. If someone carries *you where you do not wish,* you're under their authority. You follow their orders instead of your own.

So if *you will stretch out your hands, and another will gird you and carry you where you do not wish,* you have surrendered the right to do as you please and have submitted to the authority of someone else. This is the mindset you need to have in regard to serving the Lord. *Not as I will, but as He will* (Matthew 26:39). You no longer do whatever you want to do, but you do what He wants you to do. The Lord created you. Therefore, you're to be under His authority and in obedience to Him.

If you didn't submit to God when you were younger, you can do so today. At this present moment and in the future, you can submit to the Lord and be obedient to Him. You may have had a rough past and really messed up, but as long as you're alive, it's not too late to turn things around. So as long as you have breath, *present your bodies a living sacrifice, holy, acceptable to God, which is your reasonable service* (Romans 12:1).

IV. Conclusion

All of us have girded ourselves and have walked where we wished. It's in our human nature to gird and prepare ourselves to sin. *The imagination of man's heart is evil from its youth* (Genesis 8:21). It's also in our nature to practice sin and walk in sin. *Men loved darkness rather than light, because their deeds were evil* (John 3:19). People love the darkness of sin rather than the light of God's truth. However, there are consequences if we walk where we wish. *There is a way that seems right to a man, but its end is the way of death* (Proverbs 14:12).

The Pharisees and Roman soldiers girded Jesus and carried Him where He did not wish. He asked God the Father if it was possible to let the cup of His wrath pass from Him. However, He submitted to the will of the Father. He laid down His life and took on the sins of all mankind. Because of this, we can have a relationship with God through Him and walk where He wants us to go. If you have yet to do so, believe on the Lord Jesus. *Whoever believes in Him should not perish but have everlasting life* (John 3:16).

V. Discussion Questions

1. What are your initial thoughts? Is there anything that stuck out to you while reading this?

2. When you think of second chances, what comes to mind?

3. What do second chances show you in regard to the Lord and His character?

4. How can second chances give you a greater appreciation for the Lord?

5. What are some ways we can submit to the Lord today and in the future?

6. Can you think of a time when you received a second chance and were able to capitalize on it?

7. Is there anything that you can take away from this discussion and apply to your life? Any final thoughts?

Lesson 10

Called Us to His Eternal Glory

To My Sister in Christ, Kayla C.

May the God of all grace, who called us
to His eternal glory by Christ Jesus,
after you have suffered a while, perfect,
establish, strengthen, and settle you.

—1 Peter 5:10

I. Introduction

Have you ever grown in a season of adversity due to someone's help? For instance, maybe you fell into a deep depression due to the death of a loved one, but with support from family and friends, you got through it. Now you're able to comfort others who are in a similar position. Perhaps you lost your job. Although it was a low moment, your friend set you up with a new job to help you get back on your feet, and you're much happier at your new job than in your previous position.

If the answer is yes, then you have received succor. "Succor" is assistance and support in times of hardship. You encounter some sort of adversity, but someone else recognized or was informed that you were in distress. As a result, they took action to help you with your problem. With their help, you were able to get through your season of difficulty and come back stronger than before.

II. Context

In 1 Peter 5:10, the apostle Peter told the churches at Asia Minor that he hoped they would receive succor. He also talked about who could provide them with it: *the God of all grace, who called us to His eternal glory by Christ Jesus.* Peter then stated when they should receive it: *after you have suffered a while.* Peter additionally mentioned how the Lord will succor them: He will *perfect, establish, strengthen, and settle you.*

III. Main Points

Like Peter's hope for the Asia Minor church, *May the God of all grace, who called us to His eternal glory by Christ Jesus, after you have suffered a while, perfect, establish, strengthen, and settle you.* "Grace" is defined as unmerited favor. It's when you receive what you don't deserve. The Lord is the sole owner of grace, which means that it stems from Him. *Every good gift and every perfect gift is from above, and comes down from the Father of lights, with whom there is no variation or shadow of turning* (James 1:17). This indicates that the Lord gives us good things that we don't deserve.

An example of His grace is that He called us into *His eternal glory by Christ Jesus.* "Eternal glory" can be defined as something that's magnificent in quality, worthy of praise, and imperishable. The Lord wants you to be in His magnificent presence, which is worthy of all praise and is incorruptible. He wants to give us the gift of everlasting life, by which we can live with Him for eternity in the new heaven and new earth. But what have you done to deserve this gift? You have done nothing to deserve it, which is why it's known as the gift of grace.

After you have suffered a while is a prophecy of warning. *In the world you will have tribulation* (John 16:33). Sooner or later, you will have some sort of adversity in your life. Peter did not say *if* you have suffered, but he said *after* you have suffered. *Suffered a while* indicates that the tribulations you endure will be for a certain period of time. So if you're a Christian, don't expect hardship and tribulation to be an anomaly or a rare event, but expect to experience them throughout your life.

Although you will go through suffering, God can *perfect, establish, strengthen, and settle you.* To perfect means to mature and refine. God can use hardships to mature and refine you in your faith. *The testing of your faith produces patience. But let patience have its perfect work, that you may be perfect and complete, lacking nothing* (James 1:3–4). "Establish" is *stērizō* in Greek, which means to set fast (Strong's 4741). To set fast means to firmly place in a specific location. If we seek the Lord, He can set us where He wants us to be. Therefore, acknowledge Him in all your ways, and *He shall direct your paths* (Proverbs 3:6).

"Strengthen" means to increase or grow in a capability. Just as strength training helps weightlifters build physical muscles, suffering can help us build spiritual muscles. Through suffering, we can grow in godly character. *Tribulation produces perseverance; and perseverance, character; and character, hope* (Romans 5:3–4). "Settle" is *themelioō* in Greek, which means to lay a foundation for (Strong's 2311). If you listen to the Lord, He will lay a solid foundation for you. Because of this, you can remain steadfast in the faith. As Jesus said, *Whoever hears these sayings of Mine, and does them, I will liken him to a wise man who built his house on the rock: and the rain descended, the floods came, and the winds blew and beat on that house; and it did not fall, for it was founded on the rock* (Matthew 7:24–25).

IV. Conclusion

May the God of all grace [call] us to His eternal glory (1 Peter 5:10). *For all have sinned and fall short of the glory of God* (Romans 3:23). We all have broken God's law and violated His commandments. Because of our sin, we are ineligible for God's glory. We are not good enough to be in the wonderful and magnificent presence of the Lord up in heaven because He requires absolute perfection.

The good news is that God calls us into His eternal glory by Jesus Christ. Hence, we can be *justified freely by His grace through the redemption that is in Christ Jesus* (Romans 3:24). Jesus lived a perfect life, died on the cross, was buried for three days, and rose from the dead. Through Christ's death, burial, and resurrection, we can be in the magnificent presence of God. We can dwell in His eternal paradise forever and ever. Therefore, don't receive the grace of God in vain. *Now is the accepted time; behold, now is the day of salvation* (2 Corinthians 6:2).

V. Discussion Questions

1. What are your initial thoughts? Is there anything that stuck out to you while reading this?

2. When you think of "eternal glory," what comes to mind?

3. In what ways do "the God of all grace" and "called us into His eternal glory" give you a better understanding of the Lord and who He is?

4. What does "after you have suffered a while" indicate? How is this contrary to the prosperity gospel of health and wealth?

5. How can God's promise to *perfect, establish, strengthen, and settle you* help when going through trials and tribulations? Can you recall a time when this promise has helped you in a time of difficulty?

6. How can God's promise to *perfect, establish, strengthen, and settle you* give you a greater appreciation for Him?

7. Is there anything that you can take away from this discussion and apply to your life? Any final thoughts?

He Who Has Begun a Good Work in You

Dedicated to Jahmir (Market Street Mission)

Being confident of this very thing, that He who has begun a good work in you will complete it until the day of Jesus Christ.

—Philippians 1:6

I. Introduction

Think of a time when you did all the tasks you needed to do. For instance, maybe you cleaned up your room. You folded your clothes, stored them in the closet, swept the floors, washed the windows, and made your bed. Perhaps you finished your project at work. You did everything your boss required of you. Maybe you just ran a marathon. You endured the 26.2-mile race and crossed the finish line.

The scenarios above exemplify completion. Completion is when you finish a task or reach the end of an activity. In order for you to complete something, you must first decide that you will start something. Then you must continue the process. In this way, you can make progress toward completion. When you reach the end of the process, that is the point of completion.

II. Context

In Philippians 1:6, the apostle Paul completed his commendation to the church at Philippi with a promise from the Lord. Paul saw that their faith in the Lord was evident and steadfast. He was sure that the Lord would complete what He started in them: *Being confident of this very thing, that He who has begun a good work in you will complete it until the day of Jesus Christ* (Philippians 1:6).

III. Main Points

As Paul told the church at Philippi, *be confident of this very thing.* "Confident" means to be sure and to have faith in something. Be confident in the Lord's promises because whatever He says will come to pass. It is not a matter of if, but when. *Has He said, and will He not do? Or has He spoken, and will He not make it good?* (Numbers 23:19). The Lord is El Emeth: the God of Truth. You can trust whatever He says or promises since it is all truth.

Remember that it is *He who has begun a good work in you.* "He" is in reference to the Lord. "Has begun a good work in you" alludes to justification. Justification is the starting point of one's faith in the Lord, when He moves someone from a state of condemnation to one of innocence. It alludes to justification because "begun" marks the starting point of something and "a good work in you" symbolizes your faith in the Lord.

It is the Lord who begins *a good work in you. It is God who justifies* (Romans 8:33). "He" marks the beginning of your relationship with Him. He takes you from condemnation to justification. Also, He is the only one who can begin *a good work in you.* No other god or religion can give you an everlasting relationship, as well as saving faith. *[He is] the Lord, and there is no other; there is no God besides [Him]* (Isaiah 45:5).

Know that He *will complete it until the day of Jesus Christ.* This is a promise about sanctification to glorification. Sanctification is a part of the completion process in which the Lord makes you holy and more like Him in character. Glorification is the end point in which the Christian is made perfect. Glorification will happen at the day of Jesus Christ, which is His second coming. If you believe in the Lord Jesus for salvation, He will complete the good work that is in you until He returns to earth and gives you a glorified body.

IV. Conclusion

Be confident of this very thing: the gospel of Jesus Christ. We can be confident in the good news of the gospel because God cannot lie, and the Lord Jesus, who is God in the flesh, stated that He is the only way by which we can have salvation: *I am the way, the truth, and the life.* No one comes to the Father except through Me

(John 14:6). Good works and other gods can't get you into heaven, but only the Lord Jesus can.

Be confident that if you repent of your sins and believe on the Lord Jesus Christ, God will begin a good work in you. He will forgive you of the sins that you have committed against Him. *If we confess our sins, He is faithful and just to forgive us our sins and to cleanse us from all unrighteousness* (1 John 1:9). If you believe on Jesus, God will complete a good work in you. *Whoever believes in Him should not perish but have everlasting life* (John 3:16).

V. Discussion Questions

1. What stood out to you about this lesson and the passages discussed?

2. When you think of completion, what comes to mind? Why?

3. Why should you be confident that *He who has begun a good work in you will complete it until the day of Jesus Christ?*

4. What are some similarities and differences between justification, sanctification, and glorification?

5. How can the promise listed in Philippians 1:6 give you a greater appreciation for the Lord?

6. How can the promise listed in Philippians 1:6 help you in your walk with the Lord?

7. Is there anything that you can take away from this discussion and apply to your life? Any final thoughts?

To Save Sinners

To My Brother in Christ, Spencer P.

This is a faithful saying and worthy of all acceptance, that Christ Jesus came into the world to save sinners, of whom I am chief.

—1 Timothy 1:15

I. Introduction

Think of a situation in which a person has been rescued from potential danger. For example, firefighters go into a burning house to rescue those who are trapped inside. A lifeguard sees someone drowning in the sea and goes into the water to rescue the person. A policeman notices that someone is being robbed, so he intervenes to end the attack.

These situations show the act of saving. To save means to rescue someone from potential harm or danger. In order for saving to take place, someone has to be in a vulnerable position. They're in a place where they may get hurt. Also, someone has to notice the potential danger, whether that person is the person in danger or an outside party. An action also must occur in which the vulnerable person is taken out of danger.

II. Context

In 1 Timothy 1:15, Paul brought up the topic of saving. He first told his protégé Timothy that the statement he was about to make should be universally accepted by all people: *This is a faithful saying and worthy of all acceptance.* He then told him why Jesus came into the world: *that Christ Jesus came into the world to save sinners, of whom I am chief.*

III. Main Points

As Paul told Timothy, *This is a faithful saying and worthy of all acceptance.* "This" refers to the declaration that Paul made later in the verse. "Faithful" is *pistos* in Greek, which means sure and true (Strong's 4103). A faithful saying, then, is a statement that is true and credible. If a statement is true, then it's worthy of acceptance. It should be believed as valid and correct.

You can trust that the declaration Paul made later in the verse is a faithful saying because it's in Scripture. If it's in Scripture, then it is of God. *All Scripture is given by inspiration of God, and is profitable for doctrine, for reproof, for correction, for instruction in righteousness* (2 Timothy 3:16). Also, God *cannot lie* (Titus 1:2). Therefore, you can trust that His Word is true, and you should believe it. So whether it's a statement from Paul or another author, if the writing is originally found in Scripture, trust that it *is a faithful saying and worthy off all acceptance* because it is of the Lord.

Know that *Christ Jesus came into the world to save sinners.* The Lord Jesus came down from heaven for a specific purpose. He came to save those who violated God's law. He came to save them from eternal death, which is an eternity of torment in the lake of fire. Given that all people have sinned, this means that the Lord came to save you!

Christ Jesus came into the world to save sinners, of whom I am chief. "Chief" is *protos* in Greek, which means foremost, first, or best (Strong's 4413). So what Paul meant was that he was the worst sinner of them all. Nevertheless, Christ came to save him. So if you have done some terrible things in your life, don't think that you're too far gone for God to save you. If He saved Paul, who was the chief and worst of sinners, He can also save you.

IV. Conclusion

Let us remember that *this is a faithful saying and worthy of all acceptance, that Christ Jesus came into the world to save sinners.* But how did Jesus save sinners? He saved sinners through the gospel. The Lord knew that the whole world was in need of a Savior. He knew that without a Savior, the whole world would be lost. Everyone would be dead in their trespasses and sin, and everyone would be destined to hell and the lake of fire.

Therefore, Jesus took on human flesh and *dwelt among us* (John 1:14). *He was wounded for our transgressions, He was bruised for our iniquities; the chastisement for our peace was upon Him, and by His stripes we are healed* (Isaiah 53:5). Jesus laid down His life for the punishment of our sins, and He can save anyone who calls upon Him for salvation. *Whoever calls on the name of the Lord shall be saved* (Joel 2:32; Acts 2:21; Romans 10:13).

V. Discussion Questions

1. What are your initial thoughts? Is there anything that stuck out to you while reading this?

2. Why is it important to know that everything in Scripture *is a faithful saying and worthy of all acceptance*? What are some verses that can remind you of this truth?

3. How can the statement "Christ Jesus came into the world to save sinners" give you a better understanding of the gospel?

4. In what ways does the statement "Christ Jesus came into the world to save sinners" give you a greater appreciation for the Lord?

5. How can the statement "Christ Jesus came into the world to save sinners, of whom I am chief" give you and others hope?

6. Have you ever felt too far gone for God to save you? Why or why not?

7. Is there anything that you can take away from this discussion and apply to your life? Any final thoughts?

He Who Overcomes

To My Brother in Christ, George T.

He who overcomes shall inherit all things,
and I will be his God and he shall be My son.

—Revelation 21:7

I. Introduction

Have you ever been in a challenging situation and were able to get through it? Perhaps you were in the middle of a race. Your legs were burning and you were breathing heavily. Stopping would have provided immediate relief, but you pushed through and made it to the finish line. Maybe you suffered heartbreak. You felt as if your life was over and that you would never be happy again. But little by little you started to heal, and you were able to move on with your life.

These examples show you what it means to overcome. To overcome is to successfully deal with a difficult problem. "Overcome" is translated as *nikao* in Greek, which means to conquer, prevail, and have victory (Strong's 3528). In order to overcome, there must first be a problem that is in the way of your progress. Then there is the response, when you decide to deal with the problem. That is followed by the result, when you gain victory over the problem.

II. Context

In Revelation 21:7, the Lord talked about who will spend eternity with Him in the new heaven and new earth. He gave a condition and two promises. He first listed the condition of the promise: *he who overcomes*. He then stated the promises for those who overcome. The first promise is an inheritance: *shall inherit all things*. The second promise is a relationship with Him: *I will be his God and he shall be My son.*

III. Main Points

Remember the Lord's condition: *he who overcomes*. He who overcomes is the one who has prevailed against the eternal consequences of sin. He is triumphant over Satan's attempt to drag him into everlasting damnation. He is victorious over the second death, which is eternity in the lake of fire. He who overcomes shall not be hurt by the second death (Revelation 2:11).

He who overcomes shall inherit all things. To inherit means to receive something as a gift from a predecessor. A predecessor is someone who has had previous possession of something, and this usually is a parent, a family member, or a loved one. Similar to the one who inherits a gift from a parent, we also receive an inheritance from our Father in heaven.

All things are the eternal blessings of the Lord. This includes the gift of eternal life. *Whoever believes in Him should not perish but have everlasting life* (John 3:16). It includes a permanent residence in the new heaven and new earth. Overcomers will get to reside in the holy city, New Jerusalem, for eternity. *All things* also includes everlasting peace. *God will wipe away every tear from their eyes; there shall be no more death, nor sorrow, nor crying. There shall be no more pain, for the former things have passed away* (Revelation 21:4). It additionally includes blessings that are beyond man's comprehension. *Eye has not seen, nor ear heard, nor have entered into the heart of man the things which God has prepared for those who love Him* (1 Corinthians 2:9).

He who overcomes will also inherit a relationship with God. *I will be his God and he shall be My son.* There is a connection in which the Lord considers those who overcome to be His children. If you're a child of God, you will inherit characteristics and qualities that stem from Him. For instance, the Lord gives you His Spirit, which is the Holy Spirit. He guides you *into all truth* (John 16:13). With the Holy Spirit, you can walk in the ways of the Lord, which will help you overcome the challenges in your life. *He who is in you is greater than he who is in the world* (1 John 4:4). The Holy Spirit, who is in the overcomer, is greater than Satan and his demons.

IV. Conclusion

We can overcome through the Lord Jesus Christ. From the salvific aspect, he who overcomes is the one who repents and believes on the Lord Jesus Christ. *Who is he who overcomes the world, but he who believes that Jesus is the Son of God?* (1 John 5:5). Sin is the major obstacle in our lives. Everyone is guilty of sin, which has major consequences. It leads to death, as well as to eternal torment in hell and the lake of fire.

However, Jesus overcame death. He conquered, prevailed, and obtained victory over it. Through His death, burial, and resurrection, we can overcome the eternal second death. Through Him, we can overcome eternal torment in hell and the lake of fire. *O Death, where is your sting? O Hades, where is your victory?* (1 Corinthians 15:55). So if you have not yet done so, believe on the Lord Jesus Christ. Only in this way can you overcome death and hell, as well as inherit the gift of everlasting life.

V. Discussion Questions

1. What are your initial thoughts? Is there anything that stuck out to you while reading this?

2. When you think of "overcome," what comes to mind? Why?

3. How does "he who overcomes" point to the gospel?

4. In what ways can the Lord's eternal blessings show you His grace and generosity?

5. How can the Lord's promises of blessings and relationship give you a greater appreciation for Him?

6. How can the Lord's promises of blessings and relationship give you encouragement for today and hope for the future?

7. Is there anything that you can take away from this discussion and apply to your life? Any final thoughts?

What Is Love?

To My Sister in Christ, Maica P.

Love suffers long and is kind.

—1 Corinthians 13:4

I. Introduction

Think about a specific object or concept and how you would explain it. In some cases, you would express what something is through its attributes. For instance, if you were to explain what "hot" means, you may say it's something that consists of a high temperature. You can also express what something is through its functions. If you were to explain what a car is, you may talk about how it's a four-wheeled vehicle used to transport people from one place to another.

These are some examples of a definition. A definition is how you express what something is. It's the description of an entity. In order to define something, a few steps need to take place. First, there's observation, when you take a look at the entity. Then there's assessment, when you take note of its functions and features. That is followed by the conclusion, when you come to a decision on what the entity is. Finally, there is description, when you express your conclusion in words or writing.

II. Context

In 1 Corinthians 13:4–8, the apostle Paul continued his explanation to the church of Corinth about why love is more important than any spiritual gift. He provided them with a definition of what love is. Paul described love's different characteristics in detail: *Love suffers long and is kind; love does not envy; love does not parade itself, is not puffed up; does not behave rudely, does not seek its own, is not provoked, thinks no evil; does not rejoice in iniquity, but rejoices in the truth; bears all things, believes all things, hopes all things, endures all things. Love never fails.*

III. Main Points

As Paul told the church of Corinth, *love suffers long and is kind.* Longsuffering is patience in times of trouble. It's a reflection of love because it shows selflessness. You lay down any desire to complain, and you endure with patience. *Do all things without complaining and disputing, that you may become blameless and harmless, children of God without fault in the midst of a crooked and perverse generation, among whom you shine as lights in the world* (Philippians 2:14–15).

"Kind" is *chresteuomai* in Greek, which means to act benevolently and to show oneself useful (Strong's 5541). If you're kind, you have a desire to do good. When you do good, you show yourself useful. You can bless other people and help lead them to the Lord. Kindness is a characteristic of love because it shows that you care about others. *Therefore, as we have opportunity, let us do good to all, especially to those who are of the household of faith* (Galatians 6:10).

Love does not envy. To envy is to have resentful feelings because you desire to have something that isn't yours. Envy isn't love because it demonstrates selfishness. You choose to put the focus solely on yourself and your wants. Also, envy doesn't benefit other people, but is rather destructive. *Where envy and self-seeking exist, confusion and every evil thing are there* (James 3:16).

Love does not parade itself, is not puffed up. If you parade yourself and are puffed up, then you have pride. Pride is excessive self-importance. You think you're better than others, and in some cases you become your own god. Pride isn't love because you're obsessed with yourself. You exalt yourself so much that you have little to no regard for others.

Love *does not behave rudely, does not seek its own, is not provoked, thinks no evil.* Rude behavior isn't love because it damages others. When you treat people poorly, you can create physical and emotional wounds, as well as roots of bitterness. *Seek its own* isn't love because it's rooted in selfish motives. Love *is not provoked* because you sacrifice your desire to retaliate when someone angers you. *He who covers a transgression seeks love* (Proverbs 17:9). Love *thinks no evil* because of its altruistic nature. If you want what's best for people, then you will have no ill will toward them.

Love *does not rejoice in iniquity, but rejoices in the truth.* Iniquity is immoral and unjust behavior. Love can't rejoice in iniquity because it doesn't have your best interest in mind. It is sin and will lead to your demise. *The wages of sin is death* (Romans 6:23). On the other hand, truth is in alignment with reality. Love *rejoices in the truth* because it has your best interest in mind. *The truth shall make you free* (John 8:32).

Love *bears all things, believes all things, hopes all things, endures all things.* "Bear" is *stego* in Greek, which means to roof over and cover (Strong's 4722). A covering can represent protection. Protection is a characteristic of love because it provides a benefit to others. It prevents harm and destruction. *Love will cover a multitude of sins* (1 Peter 4:8). "Believe" is *pisteuo* in Greek, which means to commit and put in trust with (Strong's 4100). Love is a commitment in which you choose to stick to something. To put your trust in something demonstrates love because it shows that you value it. Can you love something that you don't value?

Hope is a belief and expectation that something desirable will take place in the future. Love *hopes all things* because it can point you to what's beneficial in the long term. To endure means to remain for an extended period of time. Love *endures all things* since you choose to care for others on a continual basis. If you continue something, it keeps on going. Therefore, if you continue to love, it will endure.

Love *never fails.* To fail means to not accomplish a goal or meet an expectation. *Love never fails* because it always glorifies God. The main reason you exist is to do what God wants you to do. What does God want you to do? He wants you to love Him *with all your heart, with all your soul, and with all your mind,* as well as to *love your neighbor as yourself* (Matthew 22:37, 39). If you obey the Lord, you will fulfill your mission in life. *Love never fails* because it's who God is. Remember, *God is love* (1 John 4:8). Also, *as for God, His way is perfect* (Psalm 18:30). If something is perfect, then it is without fault. Because *God is love* and He is always without fault, it is impossible for love to fail.

IV. Conclusion

The Lord Jesus is the epitome and premier example of love. Jesus suffered long and is kind. The Lord is *longsuffering toward us, not willing that any should perish but that all should come to repentance* (2 Peter 3:9). Jesus didn't envy anyone. The

Lord *gives to all life, breath, and all things* (Acts 17:25). Therefore, He didn't want what somebody else had, nor was He resentful of anyone else's possessions. Jesus did not parade Himself and was not puffed up. He *made Himself of no reputation, taking the form of a bondservant.* Jesus also *humbled Himself and became obedient to the point of death, even the death of the cross* (Philippians 2:7–8).

The Lord Jesus didn't behave rudely or seek His own. He wasn't easily provoked, and He thought no evil. His gospel doesn't have ulterior motives, and it certainly is not evil. It's all-inclusive in that anyone who believes in it can receive everlasting life. Jesus *does not rejoice in iniquity, but rejoices in the truth.* Remember, He is the truth (John 14:6). Jesus bore all things, believed all things, hoped all things, and endured all things. He bore all the sins of the world. He believed that the entire world could be saved through Him. His hope is for all to be saved, and He endured all sorts of persecutions from sinners. Jesus never fails because He is perfect. His gospel never fails because no one who believes in Him will die in their sins. So if you have yet to do so, *believe on the Lord Jesus Christ, and you will be saved* (Acts 16:31).

V. Discussion Questions

1. What stood out to you about this lesson and the passages discussed?

2. When you think about the different attributes of love, what comes to mind? Why?

3. Which attribute of love sticks out to you the most? Why?

4. How do the biblical attributes of love differ from society's definition of love? Why is this important to keep note of?

5. How can the different attributes of love give you a better understanding and greater appreciation of the Lord?

6. What are some ways you can apply the different attributes of love in your life today?

7. Is there anything that you can take away from this discussion and apply to your life? Any final thoughts?

The Lord Is My Shepherd

To My Sister in Christ, Becca B.

The Lord is my shepherd; I shall not want.

—Psalm 23:1

I. Introduction

Think of a scenario in which someone takes care of another person, or even an entire group of people. For instance, many parents raise their children to be mature, responsible, and healthy adults. Pet owners nurture and take care of their animals. Teachers are responsible for their students. Doctors medically supervise their patients, as well as help them recover from their ailments.

Shepherds are another example of those who take care of others. A shepherd is defined as one who herds, tends, and guards sheep. "Shepherd" is *ra'ah* in Hebrew, which means teacher, friend, companion, or pastor (Strong's 7462). To be a shepherd, one must truly care for the sheep and devote themselves entirely to their care, for the job of a shepherd is extremely demanding. The sheep are dependent on the shepherd since they get *weary and scattered* without one (Matthew 9:36).

II. Context

In Psalm 23, David talked about who his shepherd was in the figurative sense. He declared that the Lord was his shepherd: *The Lord is my shepherd.* David then mentioned a result of the Lord being his shepherd. He implied that because the

Lord was his shepherd, he was in need of nothing: *I shall not want.* Throughout the rest of the psalm, David explained why the Lord was his shepherd.

III. Main Points

The Lord gives peace. *He makes me to lie down in green pastures; He leads me beside the still waters* (Psalm 23:2). Shepherds must always be on the move to feed their sheep. If they remain in the same area, they put their flock in danger of malnourishment. However, the sheep become nervous if they are in new and unfamiliar territory. Therefore, shepherds calm their sheep down and make them *lie down in green pastures.* Sheep are also afraid of running water. Some are fearful to the point that they die of thirst rather than drink running water, so the shepherd has to lead his flock *beside the still waters.*

Just as the Lord gave the shepherds peace, so the Lord can give peace to you. He is known as the *Prince of Peace* (Isaiah 9:6), which means He is the ruler of it. His peace may help you remain stable in all situations. *The peace of God, which surpasses all understanding, will guard your hearts and minds through Christ Jesus* (Philippians 4:7). He gives you peace through the Holy Spirit. Jesus said, *Peace I leave with you, My peace I give to you; not as the world gives do I give to you. Let not your heart be troubled, neither let it be afraid* (John 14:27).

The Lord restores and leads. *He restores my soul; He leads me in the paths of righteousness for His name's sake* (Psalm 23:3). To restore means to bring back to a previous condition, especially one that was optimal. If the flock becomes weary, the shepherd must lead the sheep in the right direction. This way, they can be restored in health. Otherwise, the flock will grow weary and will scatter.

Likewise, the Lord guides you through His Word. *Your word is a lamp to my feet and a light to my path* (Psalm 119:105). He does it for His glory—*for His name's sake.* Obeying His Word can bring restoration to your life. *He who sows to his flesh will of the flesh reap corruption, but he who sows to the Spirit will of the Spirit reap everlasting life* (Galatians 6:8). Obedience to God's Word might even restore the souls of other people who might then glorify Him. Therefore, *let your light so shine before men, that they may see your good works and glorify your Father in heaven* (Matthew 5:16).

The Lord protects. *Yea, though I walk through the valley of the shadow of death, I will fear no evil; for You are with me; Your rod and Your staff, they comfort me* (Psalm 23:4). Sheep are basically defenseless and vulnerable to predators, especially if they go astray from the pack. Similarly, without the Lord, *you can do nothing* (John 15:5). He gives you the grace and strength to get through all your situations, even the most difficult ones. Because of Him, you can walk through the valley of the shadow of death. With His love, you don't have to fear evil. Remember—*perfect love casts out fear* (1 John 4:18). God's rod and staff can comfort you because He is the *God of all comfort, who comforts us in all our tribulation* (2 Corinthians 1:3–4).

The Lord provides. *You prepare a table before me in the presence of my enemies; You anoint my head with oil; My cup runs over* (Psalm 23:5). A shepherd must be attentive to the needs of the flock in order to take care of them. If a shepherd is attentive to the needs of the flock, then how much more does the Lord know the needs of His people? Remember, He is Jehovah Jireh: the Lord is My Provider. This means that provision is part of His holy character.

The Lord can provide in the midst of opposition. *You prepare a table before me in the presence of my enemies.* The Lord may also provide hospitality. *You anoint my head with oil.* While it is true that the ancient Israelites anointed with oil to inaugurate priests, prophets, and kings into their respective offices, it was also done when someone welcomed a guest into their house.[1] So even if you're in hostile territory, the Lord can make you feel right at home if that's where He wants you to be. The Lord can provide abundantly. Hence, *my cup runs over.*

The Lord is El Chuwl: the God who Gave You Life. *Surely goodness and mercy shall follow me all the days of my life; and I will dwell in the house of the Lord forever* (Psalm 23:6). Shepherds must put the needs of the sheep before their own, for in this way, the sheep have a better chance of survival. Similarly, *the good shepherd gives His life for the sheep* (John 10:11). The Lord Jesus died so that you may live. With His goodness, you're able to repent to salvation: *The goodness of God leads you to repentance* (Romans 2:4). With His mercy, you're spared from eternal death: *Through the Lord's mercies we are not consumed* (Lamentations 3:22). Instead, He can grant us eternal life and a heavenly residence. Hence, *I will dwell in the house of the Lord forever.*

IV. Conclusion

The Lord Jesus Christ can be your shepherd. *All we like sheep have gone astray* (Isaiah 53:6). We have gone away from the correct path and direction of the Lord.

---

1   "How and Why Are People Anointed with Oil?" Christianity.com, October 12, 2023, https://www.christianity.com/wiki/christian-terms/anointed-definition-anointing-oils.html.

We have erred from the path of truth and have gone in the way of error. Without a shepherd, we, like sheep, will become weary and scattered. Without Christ, we will be lost and will wither away to our demise.

But the Lord Jesus Christ is the Good Shepherd who *gives His life for the sheep* (John 10:11). He cared about the flock of mankind and laid down His life so they can come back into His fold. He died on the cross so that all of us can be a part of the flock of God through Him. If you repent of your sins and believe on the Lord Jesus for salvation, you can be a part of His flock for eternity. *My sheep hear My voice, and I know them, and they follow Me. And I give them eternal life, and they shall never perish; neither shall anyone snatch them out of My hand* (John 10:27–28).

V. Discussion Questions

1. What stood out to you about this lesson and the passages discussed?

2. Which qualities of a shepherd stick out to you the most? Why?

3. How can the qualities of a shepherd give you a better understanding of the Lord?

4. In what ways do the qualities of a sheep show you man's need for God?

5. How is the relationship between shepherd and sheep similar to the relationship between God and man?

6. Why is the Lord your shepherd?

7. Is there anything that you can take away from this discussion and apply to your life? Any final thoughts?

Holy and Blameless and above Reproach

To My Brother in Christ, Peter S.

In the body of His flesh through death, to present you holy,
and blameless, and above reproach in His sight.

—Colossians 1:22

I. Introduction

Have you ever taken something that was bad and made it into something good? Consider home renovations for example. You took a home that was rundown and transformed it into a state-of-the-art residence. What about car repairs? You fixed a broken-down vehicle, and now it's a well-oiled machine. Or how about yourself? Maybe you were in poor health, but you improved your diet and began to exercise. As a result, you're in great shape.

This is what you would call the process of amelioration. Amelioration is a transition of improvement—when something goes from bad to good. For amelioration to take place, a few events need to occur. First, there's recognition, when you notice that something isn't right. There's decision, when you choose to do something about it. Next is the repair phase, when you work on the issue. Then there's the point of completion, when you have fixed the problem, and the condition is as good as new.

II. Context

In Colossians 1:21–22, the apostle Paul described a spiritual amelioration. He told the church at Colossae that they used to be in poor condition: *And you, who once were alienated and enemies in your mind by wicked works.* He then explained how God improved their condition: *yet now He has reconciled in the body of His flesh through death, to present you holy, and blameless, and above reproach in His sight.*

III. Main Points

Like the church of Colossae, you *once were alienated and enemies in your mind by wicked works.* "Alienate" means to estrange, as well as to make distant and hostile. Before you became a Christian, your relationship with God was distant and estranged to the point that it was non-existent. You were also an enemy of God in your mind. One reason for this is that your mind is carnal in its original state. It seeks only to satisfy your human desires and has no regard for God. Remember that *the carnal mind is enmity against God; for it is not subject to the law of God, nor indeed can be* (Romans 8:7).

"By" is the method in which an action is completed. Therefore, it was through the action of wicked works that you were alienated from God and were His enemy in your mind. "Wicked works" is another term for sin. Sin brings forth destruction. *He who sows to his flesh will of the flesh reap corruption* (Galatians 6:8). Because sin brings forth corruption, it can mess up your relationships. This includes your relationship with God.

Yet now He has reconciled in the body of His flesh through death. Although you were alienated and an enemy of God, He provided a way for you to have a restored relationship with Him. He made a way through His Son, Jesus Christ. He gave up His only Son and sacrificed His body unto death. Because of this, your wicked works can be forgiven and have been atoned for.

Through Christ, God is able *to present you holy, and blameless, and above reproach in His sight.* "Holy" means set apart. The word "holy" is *hagios* in Greek, which means pure (Strong's 40). "Blameless" means innocent and without fault. "Above reproach" means free of any charges. No one can bring up anything against you. If the Lord has reconciled you to Himself, there is amelioration to your spiritual condition. He has made you pure, innocent, and free from any criticism. Remember that *if anyone is in Christ, he is a new creation; old things have passed away; behold, all things have become new* (2 Corinthians 5:17).

IV. Conclusion

Jesus was holy and blameless and above reproach throughout His thirty-three years on earth. There was not a single instance when He was in error or at fault in anything. Although Satan tried to tempt Him in the wilderness, He remained holy. Even though the Pharisees attempted to trap Him, He stayed blameless. Although His fellow countrymen, the Jews, rejected Him, He remained above reproach.

Jesus remained *holy, and blameless, and above reproach* to save all *who once were alienated and enemies in [their] mind[s] by wicked works.* If you have yet to do so, believe on the Lord Jesus. He will *present you holy, and blameless, and above reproach in His sight.* Remember—Jesus is the one *who is able to keep you from stumbling, and to present you faultless before the presence of His glory with exceeding joy* (Jude 1:24). He can keep us from stumbling all the way to hell and can present us innocent in the kingdom of heaven.

V. Discussion Questions

1. What stood out to you about this lesson and the passages discussed?

2. If you *once were alienated and enemies in your mind by wicked works*, what does this tell you about human nature and the effects of sin?

3. How can this truth show you your need for God?

4. What does *yet now He has reconciled in the body of His flesh through death* teach you in regard to the gospel?

5. When you think of *holy, and blameless, and above reproach*, what comes to mind? Why?

6. Given that it's God who makes you *holy, and blameless, and above reproach*, how can this give you a greater appreciation for Him?

7. Is there anything that you can take away from this discussion and apply to your life? Any final thoughts?

Lesson 17

My Grace Is Sufficient for You

To My Brother and Sister in Christ, James and Brittney Z.

And He said to me, "My grace is sufficient for you,
for My strength is made perfect in weakness."
Therefore most gladly I will rather boast in my infirmities,
that the power of Christ may rest upon me.

—2 Corinthians 12:9

I. Introduction

Think of a time when you wanted to get rid of something, but had to deal with it. Maybe you have annoying neighbors. You want them to move far away, but they're here to stay—so you try to be patient and civil with them. Perhaps your parents make you eat vegetables at dinner. Although you don't want to eat them, you know that vegetables are healthy, and also that you may face discipline if you don't finish your food; therefore, you eat them. Maybe you have a poor-health condition. You want to be healed of it, but it's incurable—so you learn how to live with it.

These are some examples of coping. To cope is to deal with your problems and responsibilities in a calm, as well as effective, manner. When you cope, you see something that presents itself as a challenge. You don't run away from it, nor do you deal with it in a destructive manner, but you go about it in a way that's healthy.

II. Context

In 2 Corinthians 12:8–9, Paul talked to the church at Corinth about the thorn in his flesh. He first asked the Lord to remove it: *Concerning this thing I pleaded with the Lord three times that it might depart from me.* The Lord then responded to Paul's petition with an answer and explanation: *My grace is sufficient for you, for My strength is made perfect in weakness.* Paul afterward stated how he coped with the thorn in his flesh: *Therefore most gladly I will rather boast in my infirmities, that the power of Christ may rest upon me.*

III. Main Points

Like Paul, trust that God's grace *is sufficient for you.* "Grace" is *charis* in Greek, which means benefit, favor, gift, or pleasure (Strong's 5485). If you receive God's grace, it's His gift to you. It's something you don't deserve. You benefit from it as it supports you through hardships. Because the grace of God can support you through any affliction, it is sufficient for you. It is enough to cover any need that you might have, if not more. *My God shall supply all your need according to His riches in glory by Christ Jesus* (Philippians 4:19).

Recognize that His strength *is made perfect in weakness.* God's strength is manifested in the most difficult times. One reason why He may allow you to experience difficult situations is to show you your need for His strength. All too often, we can become complacent when everything is well. When someone becomes complacent, there's a tendency to rely on his or her own strength instead of the Lord's. If you rely on your own strength, pride tends to creep in. The problem is that *pride goes before destruction* (Proverbs 16:18). It will prevent you from enduring hardship. Therefore, rely on the Lord's strength instead of your own. *Humble yourselves in the sight of the Lord, and He will lift you up* (James 4:10).

Therefore, like Paul, you can gladly boast in your infirmities, *that the power of Christ may rest upon [you].* To boast means to show a lot of satisfaction in something. Infirmities are known as physical and mental weaknesses. So to boast in your infirmities is to have satisfaction in your weaknesses. One reason to have satisfaction in your weaknesses is because doing so can be used as an opportunity for the Lord to work in you and show how great He is.

The Lord can use your infirmities to strengthen your faith. *The testing of your faith produces patience. But let patience have its perfect work, that you may be perfect and complete, lacking nothing* (James 1:3–4). The Lord can use your infirmities to strengthen the faith of others. God *comforts us in all our tribulation, that we may be able to comfort those who are in any trouble, with the comfort with which we ourselves are comforted by God* (2 Corinthians 1:4). The Lord can use your infirmities to draw others to become Christians. Having infirmities and still conducting yourself in a godly manner can be used as a testimony to other people, who may see Christ in you. So although you may have infirmities, *let your light so shine before men, that they may see your good works and glorify your Father in heaven* (Matthew 5:16).

IV. Conclusion

The grace of the Lord Jesus Christ was sufficient for Jesus Himself. Like Paul, Jesus asked to be spared from affliction. Jesus asked His Father in heaven to spare Him from the cup of judgment if there was any other way to deal with the sins of the whole world. *If it is possible, let this cup pass from Me* (Matthew 26:39). Nevertheless, Jesus did the Father's will. Through His grace, He took on false accusations, beatings, backstabbing, and mocking, as well as the punishment of man's sin against God.

Because the Lord's grace was sufficient for Him to endure the cross, His grace is sufficient for us when it comes to our salvation. *For you know the grace of our Lord Jesus Christ, that though He was rich, yet for your sakes He became poor, that you through His poverty might become rich* (2 Corinthians 8:9). Because of His grace, we can be spiritually rich and saved by faith. If you have yet to do so, please receive the grace of God and His gift of salvation today. *Behold, now is the accepted time; behold, now is the day of salvation* (2 Corinthians 6:2).

V. Discussion Questions

1. What stood out to you about this lesson and the passages discussed?

2. When you hear that the Lord's grace is sufficient for you, what comes to mind? Why?

3. How is the Lord's strength made perfect in man's weakness?

4. How can you rely on God's strength instead of your own strength?

5. In what ways can you glory in your infirmities?

6. Can you recall a time when you felt the power of Christ rest upon you? If so, please explain.

7. Is there anything that you can take away from this discussion and apply to your life? Any final thoughts?

Lesson 18

Walk by Faith, Not by Sight

To My Sister in Christ, Faith R.

For we walk by faith, not by sight.

—2 Corinthians 5:7

I. Introduction

Think about how you do certain activities in your everyday life. Take driving for example. Do you use a stick shift or do you have automatic transmission? What about communication on the phone? Do you like to call, text, or have video chats? How do you spend your time? Do you like to spend it with others or do you prefer to be alone?

These are ways you can go about certain activities. A way is a method, style, or manner in which something is completed. It's how something is done. You first decide that you will attempt an action. You then come up with a plan on how you will go about it. The way you go about something is important due to the effects it can have afterward. Different methods may lead to a difference in results, for better or worse.

II. Context

In 2 Corinthians 5:6–7, the apostle Paul continued his discussion about the earthly and heavenly bodies. Paul talked about how he and his fellow workers are physically distant from the Lord while they're in their earthly bodies: *So we are always*

77

confident, knowing that while we are at home in the body we are absent from the Lord. Paul then mentioned the way he and his fellow workers act in their earthly bodies: *For we walk by faith, not by sight.*

III. Main Points

Like Paul and his fellow workers, remember to *walk.* "To walk" is *peripateō* in Greek, which means to be occupied with and go (Strong's 4043). Be occupied in your service to the Lord. Your purpose in life is to serve Him. *I beseech you therefore, brethren, by the mercies of God, that you present your bodies a living sacrifice, holy, acceptable to God, which is your reasonable service* (Romans 12:1).

Walk by faith. "By" points to the way an action is completed. *Now faith is the substance of things hoped for, the evidence of things not seen* (Hebrews 11:1). Faith is also when you have complete trust and confidence in something. To *walk by faith* is to go in such a way that it is evident that your confidence is in the Lord. Because you trust Him, you follow His ways.

Walk by faith because it's the way you please God. *Without faith it is impossible to please Him* (Hebrews 11:6). Faith pleases God because you do His will through it. God's desire is for you to love Him. *You shall love the Lord your God with all your heart, with all your soul, and with all your mind* (Matthew 22:37). If you walk by faith, you're in obedience to the Lord, and obedience is a form of love. *If you love Me, keep My commandments* (John 14:15). Walking by faith shows God that you love Him.

The Lord has given you various ways to *walk by faith.* One way is through the Holy Spirit. God gives all believers the Holy Spirit to help guide and teach them in His ways. *But the Helper, the Holy Spirit, whom the Father will send in My name, He will teach you all things, and bring to your remembrance all things that I said to you* (John 14:26). Another way is through His Word. *Your word is a lamp to my feet and a light to my path* (Psalm 119:105).

Walk by faith, not by sight. "Sight" is *eidos* in Greek, which means "appearance" (Strong's 1491). All too often, things may appear to be a certain way when they actually aren't. *There is a way that seems right to a man, but its end is the way of death* (Proverbs 14:12). Walking by sight can lead you astray. Remember that man is in opposition to God. *The carnal mind is enmity against God; for it is not subject to the law of God, nor indeed can be* (Romans 8:7). Don't go in a certain way solely because it looks and seems right to you.

IV. Conclusion

Walk by faith through the gospel of Jesus Christ. We all have walked by sight. We have walked in the ways of unrighteousness and sin. However, walking in our own ways of lawlessness can bring about disastrous outcomes. *There is a way that seems right to a man, but its end is the way of death* (Proverbs 14:12). It will eventually lead us to death, hell, and the lake of fire.

However, the Lord Jesus paved a way where we can *walk by faith*. Through His death, burial, and resurrection, we can believe on Him for salvation and walk in His ways of righteousness. *He leads [us] in the paths of righteousness for His name's sake.* If you have yet to do so, *walk by faith* and believe on the Lord Jesus Christ. If you believe on the Lord Jesus, you can have an everlasting relationship with God, as well as live in a heavenly and incorruptible body.

V. Discussion Questions

1. What stood out to you about this lesson and the passages discussed?

2. What are the differences between walking by faith and walking by sight?

3. How does walking by faith and not by sight affect the way you live in your everyday life?

4. What are some reasons you may walk by sight?

5. What are some ways you can keep consistent in walking by faith and not by sight?

6. What are some examples from Scripture when people walked by faith and not by sight? What are some examples from Scripture when people walked by sight and not by faith? What were the end results?

7. Is there anything that you can take away from this discussion and apply to your life? Any final thoughts?

Lesson 19

Be Still

To My Brother in Christ, German G. #2

Be still, and know that I am God; I will be exalted among the nations, I will be exalted in the earth!

—Psalm 46:10

I. Introduction

Think of a time when you were in trouble, but kept it together. For instance, maybe you saw that your stocks plummeted in the past few days. Although you were tempted to pull your funds out immediately, you decided to keep them in for long-term growth. Perhaps people tried to pressure you into something you weren't interested in. Even though you may have faced backlash, you stood your ground and didn't give in.

These are a few examples of composure. Composure is the ability to be calm and poised. You're able to keep it together and have a stable frame of mind. Composure in chaos is when you're able to remain intact despite hardship. Even though things may be difficult and you feel the pressure, you don't let this consume you. Instead, you continue to be stoic through the situation.

II. Context

In Psalm 46:10, the Lord gave the sons of Korah instructions in regard to composure. He told them what to do in the midst of trouble: *Be still, and know that I am*

God. The Lord also told the sons of Korah why they should be composed. In His reasoning, He made a proclamation: *I will be exalted among the nations, I will be exalted in the earth!*

III. Main Points

Just as the Lord told the sons of Korah, we, too, should be still and know that He is God. To be still means to be calm. One way to be still is through prayer. *Be anxious for nothing, but in everything by prayer and supplication, with thanksgiving, let your requests be made known to God* (Philippians 4:6). When things look bleak, you don't need to panic. Instead, you can call out to the Lord. Cast your cares upon Him, *for He cares for you* (1 Peter 5:7).

Another way to be still is through God's peace. It is *the peace of God, which surpasses all understanding,* that *will guard your hearts and minds through Christ Jesus* (Philippians 4:7). His peace can provide relief because it can free you from the war that occurs inside your heart and mind. Your heart can deceive you and grow weary, especially during times of distress. *The heart is deceitful above all things, and desperately wicked; who can know it?* (Jeremiah 17:9). However, through the peace of God, you can remain steadfast in Him.

To know means to be aware of through observation and information. You can know God through remembrance. One of His names is Jehovah Nissi, which means "the Lord is my Banner." Banners are used to remember and celebrate special moments, whether it's a holiday, team championship, war veterans, an individual's achievements, or other things.

Likewise, there may be moments in your life when you can look back and remember when the Lord brought you through a difficult situation. You may be able to recall instances when it was only through Him that you made it. If you can dwell upon the Lord's past provision, you'll be more inclined to acknowledge Him in all your ways (Proverbs 3:6), in both present and future difficulties.

You can know God through His truth. The more you fill your mind with His Word, law, and precepts, the more you can understand Him. *Knowledge of the Holy One is understanding* (Proverbs 9:10). The more you can understand Him, the more you're able to revere Him as the Almighty God who can deliver and preserve you through trouble. You can know Him as Jehovah Magen: the Lord is My Protector and Shield.

I will be exalted among the nations, I will be exalted in the earth! To exalt means to lift up and have in high regard. "Nations" is in reference to the countries outside of Israel, especially those that oppose the Israelites and the sons of Korah. The earth points to all of creation. This proclamation indicates that the Lord will put an end to the chaos and that all will come to worship Him. *All the earth shall worship You and sing praises to You; they shall sing praises to Your name* (Psalm 66:4).

If you find yourself in trouble, know that the Lord is in control. Although things may be difficult and look bleak, there's hope in that He will bring that season to an end. *No weapon formed against you shall prosper* (Isaiah 54:17). He will work all things out for His glory. He will have victory over your adversaries, and they will have to give Him glory, whether now or later.

IV. Conclusion

You can *be still* through the Lord Jesus Christ and His gospel. Remember that the gospel is known as *the gospel of peace* (Ephesians 6:15). It is the good news that will bring spiritual, as well as everlasting, calmness in your life. Through the gospel, you can know that Jesus Christ is God. You can know that He became flesh, lived a perfect life, died on the cross for our sins, was buried for three days, and rose again.

The Lord Jesus Christ *will be exalted among the nations.* When He makes His return to the earth and establishes His thousand-year kingdom, nations around the world will come to Jerusalem to worship Him, as well as to lift up His name. The Lord Jesus Christ *will be exalted in the earth!* In the future, all of creation will lift up the name of Jesus and call Him Lord. *That at the name of Jesus every knee should bow, of those in heaven and those on earth, and of those under the earth, and that every tongue should confess that Jesus Christ is Lord, to the glory of God the Father* (Philippians 2:10–11). So if you have not yet done so, exalt the name of Jesus and believe on Him today. *Whoever believes in Him should not perish but have everlasting life* (John 3:16).

V. Discussion Questions

1. What stood out to you about this lesson and the passages discussed?

2. When you think of *Be still, and know that I am God,* what comes to mind?

3. Why is it important to be still at times? How can it help you mature in faith?

4. What are some ways that you can be still?

5. What are some ways that you can know God? How can it help you get through difficult times?

6. *I will be exalted among the nations, I will be exalted in the earth!* How can knowing that give you a better understanding and appreciation of the Lord?

7. Is there anything that you can take away from this discussion and apply to your life? Any final thoughts?

Lesson 20

Peace I Leave with You

To My Sister in Christ, Jessica G.

Peace I leave with you, My peace I give to you; not as the world gives do I give to you. Let not your heart be troubled, neither let it be afraid.

—John 14:27

I. Introduction

Do you have an item or gift that reminds you of someone or something? Perhaps you have a photo of a loved one who passed away. Whenever you see the photo, you reminisce and keep the person in the photo close in your thoughts. Maybe you received a signed autograph from a professional athlete. The autograph may help you remember that specific player. Perchance your coworkers gave you a gift before you left the company. Their gift can be a reminder of the good times you had with them.

If so, then you have a memento. A memento is an object that's kept as a reminder or souvenir of a person or event. Mementos are typically given when there's a departure between two or more parties for a significant amount of time, if not permanently. The relationship between the parties is amicable enough so that one party will give the memento as a token of the bond, and the other will cherish it.

II. Context

In John 14:27, the Lord Jesus explained to the disciples that His memento, the Holy Spirit, will help them move forward when He's no longer there in person.

Peace I leave with you, My peace I give to you. Jesus also claimed that His peace is different from the world's peace: *not as the world gives do I give to you.* The Lord then gave the disciples an exhortation: *Let not your heart be troubled, neither let it be afraid.*

III. Main Points

It is the same today as it was when the Lord told His disciples then: *Peace I leave with you, My peace I give to you.* The Lord left His peace through the Holy Spirit. Peace is a state of harmony and completeness. The Holy Spirit can provide harmony since He signifies a reconciled relationship with the Lord. The Lord only gives His Spirit to those who believe on Him. With His Spirit, *you are complete in Him* (Colossians 2:10). God is in you, where He can make you whole and provide you with everything you need. Hence, *to be spiritually minded is life and peace* (Romans 8:6).

The Holy Spirit can bring peace since *He will guide you into all truth* (John 16:13). If you are led to the truth, you can know the truth. If you know the truth, there's freedom. Hence, *the truth shall make you free* (John 8:32). It can release you from the bondage of anxiety and worry. It is able to deliver you from the lies of the devil. It can liberate you from the captivity of sin and death.

The Lord's peace is *not as the world gives.* One difference between the world's peace and God's peace is duration. The world gives peace through external means, and that peace lasts only for a season. Because it's temporal, it can depart when circumstances change. It can leave when there's failing health, financial difficulties, job loss, marriage problems, the death of a loved one, times of war, and so on. On the other end, the Lord's peace has no end. *The Lord shall endure forever* (Psalm 9:7). His attributes and character are eternal. Because peace is a part of His everlasting attributes, His peace is never-ending. If you're filled with His Spirit, His peace can sustain you regardless of the circumstances.

Another distinction between the two is quality. The Lord's peace supersedes any peace the world has to offer. He is the *Prince of Peace* (Isaiah 9:6), which means He is the king, ruler, and keeper of it. Since He is the supreme ruler of peace, His peace cannot be equaled. This includes the world's peace. Because the Lord is the keeper of peace, He is the source of it. You're able to have peace directly from the One who can *give you peace always in every way* (2 Thessalonians 3:16).

Because the Lord can give you His peace, *let not your heart be troubled, neither let it be afraid* (John 14:27). *He who is in you is greater than he who is in the world*

(1 John 4:4). The Holy Spirit is greater and more powerful than the satanic forces that reside in the world. Because the Holy Spirit is greater than any demonic opposition, you can be sure that the Lord's peace will preserve you through any trial that heads your way. Remember that *the peace of God, which surpasses all understanding, will guard your hearts and minds through Christ Jesus* (Philippians 4:7). His peace is incomprehensible to the human mind and will not allow you to be overcome by the troubles of the world.

IV. Conclusion

The Lord's peace can be left with you through the gospel. It was necessary for the Lord Jesus Christ to sacrifice Himself and die on the cross. Because of this, the peace of the Holy Spirit can come upon all believers. Nevertheless I tell you the truth. It is to your advantage that I go away; for if I do not go away, the Helper will not come to you; but if I depart, I will send Him to you (John 16:7).

After Jesus rose from the dead, He gave peace to all those who believed on Him. From the day of Pentecost in Acts up until now, He has given the Holy Spirit to all Christians. If you have not yet done so, repent and believe in the gospel of Jesus Christ. Then the Lord can give you His peace in the Holy Spirit, as well as the gift of everlasting life. *Great peace have those who love [God's] law, and nothing causes them to stumble* (Psalm 119:165).

V. Discussion Questions

1. What stood out to you about this lesson and the passages discussed?

2. What are some ways the Lord has given you His peace?

3. What are some examples from Scripture when the Lord has given peace to His people?

4. What are some differences between the world's peace and God's peace?

5. Why is it important to remember the differences between the world's peace and God's peace? What can happen if you don't discern between the two?

6. How can the peace of God keep your heart from being troubled or afraid in times of difficulty?

7. Is there anything that you can take away from this discussion and apply to your life? Any final thoughts?

The Day of Battle

To My Brother in Christ, Steve O.

The horse is prepared for the day of battle,
but deliverance is of the Lord.

—Proverbs 21:31

I. Introduction

Can you recall a time when your mental or physical abilities were put to the test? This could be because of an exam for school, a presentation at work, or competing in an athletic event or some other competition. If so, then you might be able to attest to the amount of time you put in to get ready for it. One reason people tend to prepare for a test is to increase their chances of success. It is more difficult to pass an exam if you don't study, to give a good presentation if you don't know the content, or to win a game if you don't train.

While it's important to prepare yourself for the test, it's imperative to remember that you're not in complete control of the final results. If you're not careful, you can deceive yourself and believe that the outcome depends solely on your abilities. You can prepare as much as possible, but without the Lord, *you can do nothing* (John 15:5). You can still fail the test, have a presentation go poorly, or lose a game—even if you come prepared.

II. Context

In Proverbs 21:31, King Solomon described the relationship between man and God in regard to the test of warfare. He first acknowledged man's preparation for the test. Horses likely had to be trained and conditioned by their soldiers for combat. Otherwise, the horses would be ill-prepared for battle. Hence, *the horse is prepared for the day of battle.* Solomon then shifted to the Lord's sovereignty in the results. He believed that the Lord was the one who provided protection and success in the battle: *Deliverance is of the Lord.*

III. Main Points

Like the horses, you can be prepared for the day of battle. First you need to anticipate the day of battle. *In the world you will have tribulation* (John 16:33). No one in the history of mankind has gone through life without a single trial. Sooner or later, you will encounter trouble. You will find yourself in opposition to the armies of Satan and his forces of darkness. It's not *if* it will happen, but only a matter of *when.*

If you don't anticipate and expect the day of battle, more often than not, you'll be caught off guard. If you're caught off guard, you'll have a harder time in the day of battle. You won't be as prepared for combat, and it will be harder to persevere in the midst of it. Therefore, *be sober, be vigilant; because your adversary the devil walks around like a roaring lion, seeking whom he may devour* (1 Peter 5:8). Always be on guard because the enemy can attack at any moment—especially when you least expect it.

After you anticipate the day of battle, you can then equip yourself for it. In this way, you will have the necessary components to engage in battle. One way to equip yourself is through the Word of God. *All Scripture is given by inspiration of God, and is profitable for doctrine, for reproof, for correction, for instruction in righteousness, that the man of God may be complete, thoroughly equipped for every good work* (2 Timothy 3:16–17). Because His Word instructs you in righteousness, you can use it to combat lawlessness and wickedness. Since His Word is profitable for correction, you can know the truth and increase in discernment. With discernment, you're able to sift out the lies and avoid the traps that it may present.

You can also equip yourself through prayer. God uses prayer to strengthen your faith in Him. *Be anxious for nothing, but in everything by prayer and supplication, with thanksgiving, let your requests be made known to God* (Philippians 4:6). You can choose not to drown yourself in worry and doubt. Instead, you can go to the Lord, especially when battle arises. It's a way to show humility before Him and acknowledge that you need Him in every aspect of your life. Therefore, *humble yourselves in the sight of the Lord, and He will lift you up* (James 4:10).

After you have anticipated and equipped yourself for the day of battle, trust that *deliverance is of the Lord.* Deliverance represents rescue and safety. Although you can anticipate and prepare yourself for the day of battle, it's the Lord who rescues you and provides safety in the midst of it. He can rescue you with His grace. *His grace is sufficient,* for His strength *is made perfect in weakness* (2 Corinthians 12:8–9). He may not deliver you from all harm, but He can give you enough of His strength to endure it. He can get you through the battle, even if it appears to be all doom and gloom.

The Lord provides safety through trust. *Whoever trusts in the Lord shall be safe* (Proverbs 29:25). There is spiritual security in trusting in the Lord. You can be confident that He will supply you with all your needs in the day of battle. *My God shall supply all your need according to His riches in glory by Christ Jesus* (Philippians 4:19). You can be sure that He's in control, regardless of how difficult your battles may be. You can rely on the fact that He's able to do all things and that there is no battle that's too big for Him.

IV. Conclusion

Only the Lord Jesus Christ can deliver you from the ultimate day of battle. He can save you from the battle of sin and death. Satan's goal is to destroy your life with sin and end it with death. Not only does he want to end your life on earth, but he also wants you to suffer forever. He wants to drag you and as many other souls as possible to the pit of hell.

However, through the Lord Jesus Christ, we don't need to suffer such a horrific fate. Through His death, burial, and resurrection, we can be delivered from our sins. He is *the Lamb of God who takes away the sin of the world!* (John 1:29). Through repentance and faith, we can be delivered from the second death, which is everlasting torment in the lake of fire. If you have yet to do so, believe on the Lord Jesus Christ. *Whoever believes in Him should not perish but have everlasting life* (John 3:16).

V. Discussion Questions

1. What stood out to you about this lesson and the passages discussed?

2. In what ways do you anticipate and expect the day of battle?

3. What are some reasons that someone may be caught off guard? If you're caught off guard, how do you get back on track?

4. How have you equipped yourself for the day of battle? In what ways has doing so helped you engage in combat?

5. How can you really trust that *deliverance is of the Lord?* Why is this important to remember in the day of battle?

6. What are some verses and examples from Scripture that can remind you that *deliverance is of the Lord?*

7. Is there anything that you can take away from this discussion and apply to your life? Any final thoughts?

Trust in the Lord

To My Brother and Sister in Christ, Brendan T. and Ms. Dorice

Trust in the Lord with all your heart, and lean not on your own understanding; in all your ways acknowledge Him, and He shall direct your paths.

—Proverbs 3:5–6

I. Introduction

Has there been a time when you had to depend on someone or something for a desired outcome? Perhaps you had to rely on your teammates to win a game. Maybe you counted on your parents or guardians to drive you to school. There is a good chance that you depended on your car or another form of transportation to get you to work and back. There's a possibility that you banked on your GPS to lead you to a destination.

This is in essence what it means to trust. To trust is to place your confidence in someone or something. If you trust, you may classify a particular source as reliable. You think that it will yield a desired outcome. Because you believe that it will yield a desirable outcome, you decide to count on it. Everyone has their trust in something, whether they realize it or not. So ask yourself: Who do you trust?

II. Context

In Proverbs 3:5–6, King Solomon provided guidance to the young and told them how much they should trust in the Lord: *Trust in the Lord with all your heart.*

He then warned his audience on what not to trust: *lean not on your own understanding.* Solomon next went more in-depth on how to trust the Lord: *In all your ways acknowledge Him.* He finished his statement with a promise from the Lord: *and He shall direct your paths.*

III. Main Points

Just as Solomon urged the youth, so you should *trust in the Lord with all your heart.* You can place your full confidence in the Lord because *His way is perfect* (Psalm 18:30). He is omniscient because He *knows all things* (1 John 3:20). Because He is omniscient, He's the only one who knows all truth. Since the Lord knows all truth, there is no error in His counsel. He knows the right course of action at all times. His wisdom will never fail nor waver, regardless of the circumstances.

The Lord also desires the best for you. He has *thoughts of peace and not of evil, to give you a future and a hope* (Jeremiah 29:11). This doesn't mean that you won't have any difficulties in life, but it does mean that *He cares for you* (1 Peter 5:7) and has your best interests in mind. The Lord knows what you need, and He knows when you need it. He can use the situations in your life to draw you closer to Him, as well as to bring Him glory.

To trust in the Lord with all your heart, *lean not on your own understanding.* Don't rely solely on yourself, because it's human nature to oppose God. *The heart is deceitful above all things, and desperately wicked* (Jeremiah 17:9). The heart represents your spiritual and emotional core. Because man's heart is consistently in rebellion against the laws of God, your heart can deceive you. It can take you in a direction that's contrary to His commands. It can have you believe that you know better than God.

It is very dangerous to follow your heart. *He who trusts in his own heart is a fool* (Proverbs 28:26). Because your heart will eventually lead you astray, there's a good chance it will bring you to a dead end and a screeching halt. It will cause you to make poor decisions that could destroy your life, as well as the lives of those around you. Hence, *there is a way that seems right to a man, but its end is the way of death* (Proverbs 14:12).

Also, you need to acknowledge Him *in all your ways.* "Acknowledge" is *yāda'* in Hebrew, which means to consider (Strong's 3045). The Lord is El Emeth: the God of Truth. Since He is the God of all truth and wants what's best for you, it would be wise for you to consider Him in every aspect of your life. He should be the reason behind every decision you make. His Word should be the basis for what you do and why you do it.

If you acknowledge the Lord in all your ways, *He shall direct your paths.* The Lord will lead you if you follow Him. *Your word is a lamp to my feet and a light to my path* (Psalm 119:105). Through His Word, He can impart to you His wisdom and knowledge. He can provide you with insight on what steps to take and how to go about it. With His Spirit, *He will guide you into all truth* (John 16:13). He is able to give you the discernment to make wise decisions and avoid foolish ones.

IV. Conclusion

Trust in the Lord Jesus Christ with all your heart. Jesus trusted God the Father with all His heart. Jesus said, The Son can do nothing of Himself, but what He sees the Father do; for whatever He does, the Son also does in like manner (John 5:19). He trusted His Father, even when it cost Him His life. *And being found in appearance as a man, He humbled Himself and became obedient to the point of death, even the death of the cross* (Philippians 2:8).

On the other hand, we have all leaned on our own understanding. We have all gone our own way and sinned against God. Because of our sin, we should face everlasting punishment in hell and the lake of fire. But because the Lord Jesus trusted in God the Father with all His heart and was obedient unto death, we don't have to face such consequences. So if you have not yet done so, acknowledge Him in all your ways. Repent of your sins and put your trust in the Lord Jesus Christ. If you do, He will direct your paths with the gift of the Holy Spirit and will lead you into everlasting life.

V. Discussion Questions

1. What stood out to you about this lesson and the passages discussed?

2. When you think of *trust in the Lord with all your heart,* what comes to mind?

3. How can you *trust in the Lord with all your heart?*

4. How does *trust in the Lord with all your heart* go hand in hand with *lean not on your own understanding?*

5. What are some ways you can avoid leaning on your own understanding?

6. Why is it important to acknowledge the Lord in all your ways? When you have acknowledged Him, how has He directed your paths?

7. Is there anything that you can take away from this discussion and apply to your life? Any final thoughts?

Lesson 23

Thoughts of Peace and Not of Evil

To My Brother in Christ, Brian C.

For I know the thoughts that I think toward you, says the Lord,
thoughts of peace and not of evil, to give you a future and a hope.

—**Jeremiah 29:11**

I. Introduction

Have you ever been in a difficult situation that you really wanted to get out of? Perhaps you have been sick for a while and want to be healed. Maybe you're in a toxic work environment and you long to have another job. Maybe you don't like your family and want to get far away from them. At times, you may be able to get out of a tough spot. However, there are other instances when you may have to stick it out.

If you're in the middle of a difficult situation, know that there's hope. Hope is a combination of desire and expectation. The desire is for something to occur. The expectation is the possibility that it will actually happen. If you have hope in the midst of a difficult situation, you'll likely have a desire for better days, as well as an expectation for those days to come, whether it's sooner or later.

II. Context

In Jeremiah 29:10–11, the prophet Jeremiah gave the Israelites a message of hope. Jeremiah previously informed the Israelites that the false prophets lied to them and they wouldn't be immediately released from Babylonian captivity. He told them that the Lord would let them return to their homeland after seventy years in exile. *For thus says the Lord: After seventy years are completed at Babylon, I will visit you and perform My good word toward you, and cause you to return to this place.* Jeremiah then assured the Israelites that the Lord still cared for them: *For I know the thoughts that I think toward you, says the Lord, thoughts of peace and not of evil, to give you a future and a hope.*

III. Main Points

Just as with the Israelites facing exile in Babylon, the Lord knows the thoughts that He thinks toward you. If you are in the midst of a trying season and there seems to be no signs of deliverance, don't think that the Lord has forgotten about you. He's omniscient, which means He *knows all things* (1 John 3:20). He knows everything that takes place in your life. He knows all that you've been through. He knows exactly how you feel.

The Lord may allow you to be in a difficult season for a certain period of time, and it may be for a particular reason. *To everything there is a season, a time for every purpose under heaven* (Ecclesiastes 3:1). Sometimes hardships could be due to misconduct, and the Lord may chastise you to get you back on track. In other instances, it can be a trial, when your faith in the Lord is tested. Regardless of the reason, God can use your difficult situations to draw you closer to Him, as well as to bring Him glory.

Also, the Lord's thoughts toward you are *thoughts of peace and not of evil.* Remember that it is not God, but it is the devil who *walks about like a roaring lion, seeking whom he may devour* (1 Peter 5:8). God doesn't devise plans to cause you to stumble, nor does He try to make your life miserable. He doesn't take joy when you fall, nor does He rejoice when you're in pain. So if the Lord doesn't remove you from a bad situation, don't be deceived and think that He hates you or no longer cares about you.

In fact, God is Jehovah Shalom: the Lord Is My Peace. He desires to bring you to a place of restoration, as well as of harmony, whether it's in this life or the afterlife. He sees the bigger picture while you can only see a speck of it. While a difficult season may be hard to endure, *trust in the Lord with all your heart, and lean not on your own understanding* (Proverbs 3:5). With His Spirit, He can give you the ability to persevere and make it through hardship—and through Him, you can be calm in the midst of it.

Additionally, the Lord's plan is *to give you a future and a hope*. The Lord knows what is ideal for you, and He has your best interests in mind. *All things work together for good to those who love God, to those who are the called according to His purpose* (Romans 8:28). He knows how to use the difficulties in your life to help you in the long run. Therefore, *glory in tribulations, knowing that tribulation produces perseverance; and perseverance, character; and character, hope* (Romans 5:3–4).

With hope, you can cling to the eternal promises of God and the truth of His Word. You can also look forward to the future that He has in store for those who love Him. There's hope in that your difficult season is temporary and won't last forever. Better days lie ahead, and there's light at the end of the tunnel. So *let us run with endurance the race that is set before us, looking unto Jesus, the author and finisher of our faith* (Romans 12:1–2).

IV. Conclusion

The Lord God has thoughts of peace in the gospel. He sent His Son, Jesus Christ, to bring reconciliation between man and Him. His intentions were to bring harmony between both parties. With the gospel, the Lord has thoughts of peace since it provides eternal life. It is only through Jesus that we can receive an incorruptible glorified body in which there is freedom from death and suffering.

The Lord doesn't have thoughts of evil in the gospel. He doesn't want anyone to die in their sins. He doesn't want a single soul to be condemned and burn in everlasting fire for eternity. Instead, He *is longsuffering toward us, not willing that any should perish but that all should come to repentance* (2 Peter 3:9). He wants everyone to be saved from His wrath. So if you have not done so, *believe on the Lord Jesus Christ, and you will be saved* (Acts 16:31). You will be saved from the wrath of God and will receive the gift of everlasting life.

V. Discussion Questions

1. What stood out to you about this lesson and the passages discussed?

2. When you hear that the Lord knows the thoughts He thinks toward you, what comes to mind?

3. If you're in a difficult situation, how can you remind yourself that the Lord hasn't forgotten about you?

4. How can the Lord's *thoughts of peace and not of evil* help you in a difficult season?

5. In what ways can you be deceived and believe that the Lord has thoughts of evil and not of peace toward you?

6. How does the Lord's desire *to give you a future and a hope* increase your appreciation for Him? In what ways does this truth tie into the gospel?

7. Is there anything that you can take away from this discussion and apply to your life? Any final thoughts?

Lesson 24

My Soul Silently Waits

To My Brother in Christ, Mike Z.

Truly my soul silently waits for God;
from Him comes my salvation.

—Psalm 62:1

I. Introduction

There are times where you are anticipating something arriving. Perhaps it's an item that you've ordered online. Maybe it's a return on an investment that you've made. You could be anticipating a reply from a friend to your text. You're sure that it will come in due time. You may not know the exact date or hour it will arrive, but you're confident that sooner or later, you'll receive it.

This is what it means to silently wait. To wait means to be on standby with the expectation or hope that you will receive something. To wait silently means you're able to do so in a stable frame of mind. You're not in a state of unease or panic. Instead, you're confident, and therefore at peace, while you patiently wait for the arrival of something you hope will come.

II. Context

In Psalm 62, David stated that he quietly waited for the Lord. In this particular psalm, he wasn't worked up, but he was still and was waiting for the arrival of his king. *Truly my soul silently waits for God.* David then listed numerous reasons why he silently waited for the Lord. As his rationale, he went back and forth between the reliability of God and the unreliability of man.

III. Main Points

David silently waited because he was confident that God would save Him. *From Him comes my salvation.* Like David, the Lord can preserve you in the midst of trouble. He is able to rescue you and deliver you from it. If you can be confident in the Lord's ability to get you through times of difficulty, then you can be calm while you wait for Him to do so. *Be still, and know that I am God* (Psalm 46:10).

You can be confident to the point that you solely rely on the Lord, and no one else, for provision. *He only is my rock and my salvation* (Psalm 62:2). You should only rely on the Lord God of Israel because He is the one true God. *For there is none like You, nor is there any God besides You* (2 Samuel 7:22). It's only through Him that you can be protected, preserved, and delivered. He knows all that goes on at any given time, and He keeps watch over you. You *shall not be greatly moved* (Psalm 62:2).

David silently waited because God would eventually execute justice. *How long will you attack a man?* (Psalm 62:3). Even though the Lord is longsuffering, patient, and slow to anger, there is only so much He will tolerate. There will come a time when He will *render to each one according to his work* (Psalm 62:12). He will judge the works of all men, whether it's now or in the life hereafter. So if you practice wickedness like David's opposition, *you shall be slain, all of you like a leaning wall and a tottering fence* (Psalm 62:3). Sooner or later your misconduct will come back to haunt you.

It's possible to wait in silence because there's peace when you trust that God will set everything in order. What separates the God of Israel from everybody else is that He can see the thoughts and motives of people. *Man looks at the outward appearance, but the Lord looks at the heart* (1 Samuel 16:7). Because He can see the inner motives of man, it's impossible to fool Him. He is able to see those who *delight in lies; they bless with their mouth, but they curse inwardly* (Psalm 62:4). Since God can't be fooled, He will execute judgment to the lawless if they don't repent.

David silently waited because God is trustworthy. *Trust in Him at all times, you people* (Psalm 62:8). You can rely on the Lord in each and every situation. All too often, people only trust Him with the small ordeals or only look to Him when they're in trouble. So remember that the Lord provides everything you need in life.

Otherwise, you'll look elsewhere instead of to the Creator Himself to provide for you. Therefore, keep in mind that *my God shall supply all your need according to His riches in glory by Christ Jesus* (Philippians 4:19).

Because the Lord is trustworthy, you can go to Him in prayer. *Pour out your heart before Him* (Psalm 62:8). Whatever your concerns, troubles, or worries are, tell the Lord about them. One reason is that it is not healthy to keep your problems to yourself or bottle them inside. Doing so will lead to unnecessary stress, anxiety, and unrest. However, when you come to the Lord, the burden and weight can be lifted off you. There is a sense of relief when you're able to communicate your problems to others, especially to the Lord. So *be anxious for nothing, but in everything by prayer and supplication, with thanksgiving, let your requests be made known to God* (Philippians 4:6).

David silently waited for God because he couldn't depend on earthly possessions. *Surely men of low degree are a vapor, men of high degree are a lie* (Psalm 62:9). It doesn't matter how rich or poor someone is. Their earthly wealth is as nothing in comparison to the riches of God. It cannot compare or even come close to His glory and majesty. Hence, *they are altogether lighter than vapor* (Psalm 62:9). Material wealth is temporary, but spiritual wealth is eternal and forever. *We brought nothing into this world, and it is certain we can carry nothing out* (1 Timothy 6:7).

He who trusts in his riches will fall (Proverbs 11:28). Not only can you fall financially, but you can also fall from a peaceful state of mind. You can't always silently wait and depend on something that's perishable since it can flee at any given moment. You'll eventually be in a state of uncertainty if you invest all of your hope into it. Therefore, *if riches increase, do not set your heart on them* (Psalm 62:10).

David silently waited because the Lord is omnipotent. *Power belongs to God* (Psalm 62:11). He is the one who reigns supreme and is able to do all things. *Whatever the Lord pleases He does, in heaven and in earth, in the seas and in all deep places* (Psalm 135:6). Knowing that the Lord is the all-powerful God, you can silently wait for Him. You can calmly stand by and know that He's in control no matter how dire your situation may be.

David silently waited because God is merciful. *Also to You, O Lord, belongs mercy; for You render to each one according to his work* (Psalm 62:12). Mercy is when you don't get what you deserve. You and all of mankind have sinned against God. Sin is the violation of God's law. If God were to render to you what you deserve, you would receive eternal death. *The wages of sin is death* (Romans 6:23).

However, He doesn't want to sentence anyone, including you, to eternal death. *Through the Lord's mercies we are not consumed, because His compassions fail not* (Lamentations 3:22).

IV. Conclusion

There were occasions when Jesus silently waited in order to fulfill the Lord's will. At the end of Jesus's earthly ministry, He silently waited and didn't reply when people made false accusations against Him to Caiaphas, the high priest, as well as to the Sanhedrin. Jesus silently waited and opened not His mouth when King Herod interrogated Him. He waited and kept silent when the chief priests and elders made false accusations against Him to Pontius Pilate.

Jesus silently waited because from Him would come our salvation (Psalm 62:1). Jesus endured much hostility from sinners and endured the cross, dying for the sins of the whole world. Jesus was buried and silently waited for God to raise Him up on the third day. Hence, we don't have to die in our sins, but can be saved from eternal damnation through Him. If you have not yet done so, repent and call upon the name of the Lord Jesus Christ, for *whoever calls on the name of the Lord shall be saved* (Joel 2:32; Acts 2:21; Romans 10:13).

V. Discussion Questions

1. What stood out to you about this lesson and the passages discussed?

2. What are some reasons you silently wait for the Lord?

3. In what ways can it be difficult to silently wait for the Lord?

4. How can you counter these difficulties?

5. How can silently waiting increase your appreciation of the Lord?

6. In what ways can silently waiting help you mature in faith?

7. Is there anything that you can take away from this discussion and apply to your life? Any final thoughts?

Lesson 25

Yesterday, Today, and Forever

To My Sister in Christ, Emily M. #2

Jesus Christ is the same yesterday, today, and forever.

—Hebrews 13:8

I. Introduction

Have you ever tried to stay consistent in character regardless of the circumstances? Many people can attest to how difficult that can be, given that life isn't a constant. *You do not know what a day may bring forth* (Proverbs 27:1). People tend to be creatures of habit and desire what's predictable. When you're in an unfamiliar or difficult situation, you can be tempted to act out of character in response to it.

Although it's tempting to allow your conduct to be contingent on the situation, it would be wise to practice consistency and behavior that's pleasing to the Lord. What does it mean to be consistent? To be consistent means to behave or act in a predictable manner. It's to stay unwavering in what you do. To be consistent in well-doing and godliness is wise because it's an attribute of a Christian. You're to be steadfast in the faith since a double-minded man is *unstable in all his ways* (James 1:8).

II. Context

In Hebrews 13:8, the author talked to the Christian Jews about the consistent nature of the Lord Jesus Christ. He told them that the Lord is unwavering at all times. He first stated that the Lord was steadfast in the past. The author then mentioned that He is consistent in the present. He also proclaimed that the Lord will be the same in the future and for all eternity. *Jesus Christ is the same yesterday, today, and forever.*

III. Main Points

In order to remain consistent in holiness, you should follow the Lord Jesus Christ, who is the premier example of consistency. He *is the same yesterday.* The Lord Jesus was there from the start, for *in the beginning was the Word, and the Word was with God, and the Word was God* (John 1:1). From the beginning, He loved righteousness and hated wickedness (Psalm 45:7). All throughout the Old Testament, the Lord sustained and provided for those who put their trust in Him. He may have tested them and allowed them to go through hardship, but He eventually blessed them, whether physically or spiritually.

On the other hand, the Lord repaid those who practiced lawlessness. They may have enjoyed their sin for a season, but sooner or later, the Lord executed judgment against those who violated His law. He consistently chastised Israel for disobedience, wiped out pagan nations, and even once flooded the entire world for their wickedness. He also sent the angels who rebelled against Him, as well as anyone who rejected Him, into the pit of hell, reserved for the final judgment.

Jesus Christ *is the same today.* Although you're no longer under the Old Testament law and are in the age of grace, the Lord is still El Hakkadosh: the Holy God. He is set apart because He remains without sin, and *His way is perfect* (Psalm 18:30). Because He is a holy God, He commands you to be holy, as well as to live righteously. His grace doesn't give you license to sin, and He will severely judge those who take His grace for granted. *Do you not know that the unrighteous will not inherit the kingdom of God? Do not be deceived. Neither fornicators, nor idolaters, nor adulterers, nor homosexuals, nor sodomites, nor thieves, nor covetous, nor drunkards, nor revilers, nor extortioners will inherit the kingdom of God* (1 Corinthians 6:9–10).

Thankfully, the Lord Jesus has been consistently gracious. He has provided all New Testament believers with the gift of the Holy Spirit, who can lead you in the path of righteousness, as well as in the ways of holiness. He is the Helper who *will teach you all things, and bring to your remembrance all things that I said to you* (John 14:26). He will put into your memory what the Lord has said to you through the Word of God. The Holy Spirit can also sanctify and make you whole again. You can be filled with His *love, joy, peace, longsuffering, kindness, goodness, faithfulness, gentleness, [and] self-control* (Galatians 5:22–23).

Jesus Christ is *the same forever.* "*I am the Alpha and the Omega, the Beginning and the End,*" says the Lord, "*who is and who was and who is to come, the Almighty*" (Revelation 1:8). The Lord has always possessed eternal and everlasting attributes, and He will continue to do so for all eternity. Given that *the truthful lip shall be established forever* (Proverbs 12:19) and that His *word is truth* (John 17:17), His Word will last forever. Governments may try to ban it, apostate churches might replace it with false heresies, and scientists may attempt to disprove it, but the facts remain the same: *Heaven and earth will pass away, but My words will by no means pass away* (Matthew 24:35).

The Lord Jesus will remain supreme over all things. There will come a time when *the kingdoms of the world have become the kingdoms of our Lord and of His Christ, and He shall reign forever and ever!* (Revelation 11:15). Soon enough, the Lord Jesus will come down from heaven, establish His kingdom, and eventually usher in the new heaven and the new earth. *He shall judge the world in righteousness, and He shall administer judgment for the peoples in uprightness* (Psalm 9:8). He will eradicate all sin with His holiness, and everyone will know that He is the *King of kings and Lord of lords* (1 Timothy 6:15).

IV. Conclusion

The gospel of Jesus Christ is the same yesterday. The Old Testament is filled with more than three hundred messianic prophecies about Jesus Christ. There were prophesies of His first coming hundreds and even thousands of years before it took place. Around two thousand years ago, Jesus came down to the earth in human form, lived a perfect life, died for the punishment of our sins, was buried for three days, and rose again.

The gospel is the same today. Jesus's death is chronologically applicable. He didn't just die for Old Testament believers, but He also died for New Testament Christians. If we today *repent and believe in the gospel* (Mark 1:15), we can be saved through Him. The gospel will be the same forever. Anyone who believes on the Lord Jesus Christ will receive incorruptible glorified bodies. They will live with Him forever in the new heaven and new earth. *Whoever believes in Him should not perish but have everlasting life* (John 3:16).

V. Discussion Questions

1. What stood out to you about this lesson and the passages discussed?

2. When you hear of the Lord's consistency in the past, what comes to mind?

3. How can the Lord's consistency in the past give you a better understanding of Him?

4. In what ways can the Lord's consistency in the present help you grow in faith today? How can it draw you to be more like Him?

5. How can the Lord's everlasting consistency give you hope for the future?

6. In what ways can the Lord's everlasting consistency give you a greater appreciation for Him?

7. Is there anything that you can take away from this discussion and apply to your life? Any final thoughts?

Lesson 26

Not Everyone

To My Brother in Christ, Julio R.

Not everyone who says to Me, "Lord, Lord," shall enter the kingdom of heaven, but he who does the will of My Father in heaven.

—Matthew 7:21

I. Introduction

Have you ever thought that you were a part of something—only to find out that you weren't? Maybe you thought that you were next in line for a promotion at work, but got passed over. Maybe you were confident that you made the team, but didn't make the cut. Perhaps you anticipated that you would go to a wedding, but didn't get invited.

The scenarios above are examples of misbelief. Misbelief is an incorrect thought or opinion. You think something is true, but it actually isn't. You perceive that things are a certain way when in reality, they aren't. Misbelief tends to occur when you're overconfident. When you're overconfident, there's a tendency to overlook matters without careful examination. If you overlook details, you can jump to erroneous assumptions, which may lead to false conclusions.

II. Context

In Matthew 7:21–23, Jesus addressed the topic of misbelief. He warned His disciples against false profession. In His warning, He talked about those who incorrectly thought that they would be in heaven: *Not everyone who says to Me, "Lord, Lord," shall enter the kingdom of heaven, but He who does the will of My Father in heaven.* Jesus also provided an example of those who falsely professed faith: *Many will say to Me in that day, "Lord, Lord, have we not prophesied in Your name, cast out demons in Your name, and done many wonders in Your name?"* Jesus then gave the final verdict of the false professors, as well as His reasoning: *And then I will declare to them, "I never knew you; depart from Me, you who practice lawlessness!"*

III. Main Points

As Jesus said, *Not everyone who says to Me, "Lord, Lord," shall enter the kingdom of heaven.* One reason is due to the misbelief that you are who you say you are. The concept is that if you profess to be a Christian, then it automatically means you're a Christian. Even though profession may be a strong indicator of authentic faith, it doesn't always mean so. If you weigh 200 pounds, but say that you're 175 pounds, does that mean you are 175 pounds? If you're a biological man and claim to be a woman, are you now a biological woman? If you're 5'8" and state that you're 6'4"—are you actually that tall?

The answer to those questions is no, and the reason is due to the lack of attributes. If you don't have the qualities of something, then you can't classify yourself as that. You can't be 175 pounds if you weigh 200 pounds, you can't be a biological woman if you're biologically a male, and you can't be 6'4" if you're 5'8". The same concept applies to Christianity, in which someone of genuine faith will possess the attributes of a believer. For instance, the fruit of the Spirit will be evident in the life of a Christian. Christians will show *love, joy, peace, longsuffering, kindness, goodness, faithfulness, gentleness, [and] self-control* (Galatians 5:22–23).

Another reason why not all who call Jesus "Lord" will enter heaven is because of the misbelief that good works will get you into heaven. *Many will say to Me in that day, "Lord, Lord, have we not prophesied in Your name, cast out demons in Your name, and done many wonders in Your name?"* The mantra is that as long as you're a nice person and do good deeds, then God will let you into heaven. He will be impressed with your body of work, and you'll find yourself in His good graces.

While the ideology of "earn your way" is prevalent in the world, it's not biblical in the context of salvation. Remember: *whoever shall keep the whole law, and yet stumble in one point, he is guilty of all* (James 2:10). Because of sin, you stand guilty before God and can't work your way into heaven. So if you think your works can get you into heaven, you'll be in for a rude awakening. *And then I will declare to them, "I never knew you; depart from Me, you who practice lawlessness!"* You'll be denied access into the kingdom of heaven, and the Lord will point to your sin as the reason why.

Instead, do *the will of My Father in heaven.* The "will of My Father in heaven" can be seen as the desires of God. One reason you should do God's will is because it's a way to show your love for Him. The first and great commandment is to *love the Lord your God with all your heart, with all your soul, and with all your mind* (Matthew 22:37). You can show your love for God through obedience. *If you love Me, keep My commandments* (John 14:15). If you do what the Lord wants you to do, you can show your love for Him and fulfill His purpose for you.

A second reason you should do the Father's will is because it's the only way to enter the kingdom of heaven. God's plan of salvation doesn't align with universalism, where all roads lead to home. There is only one way to everlasting paradise, and that's through the Lord Jesus Christ. *I am the way, the truth, and the life. No one comes to the Father except through Me* (John 14:6).

IV. Conclusion

If you have yet to do the will of the Father in heaven, the most important step is to repent of your sins and put your faith in the Lord Jesus Christ today. God's desire is for all people to come to Him—and that includes you. He is *not willing that any should perish but that all should come to repentance* (2 Peter 3:9). That is why God sent His Son, Jesus, to die on the cross. No one has to die in their sins.

Through Jesus's death, burial, and resurrection, we can enter the kingdom of heaven through Him. We can say, *Lord, Lord,* and enter the kingdom of heaven because *he who does the will of God abides forever* (1 John 2:17). We can abide with Him in the third heaven, reign with Him in the millennial kingdom, and dwell with Him in the new heaven and new earth for all of eternity.

V. Discussion Questions

1. What stood out to you about this lesson and the passages discussed?

2. When you hear, *Not everyone who says to Me, "Lord, Lord," shall enter the kingdom of heaven*, what comes to mind?

3. How can this warning give you a better understanding of who God is?

4. What are some common misbeliefs? Why?

5. How can you avoid and combat misbelief?

6. What are some ways you can do *the will of My Father in heaven*?

7. Is there anything that you can take away from this discussion and apply to your life? Any final thoughts?

Fearfully and Wonderfully Made

To My Sisters in Christ, Julia S. and Tori M.

I will praise You, for I am fearfully and wonderfully made;
marvelous are Your works, and that my soul knows very well.

—Psalm 139:14

I. Introduction

Think of a time when you made something. Perhaps you baked a dessert, set up a home gym, designed some clothing, composed a song, or knitted a blanket. There's a good chance you can attest to how much detail goes into what you make. First, you need to know how to make the item. You can't finish something if you don't know what it takes to make it. Then you have to get the necessary components to complete the job. Once you have the required materials, you proceed to make the item.

This is the process of creation. To create means to form something into existence. You combine a series of components and use them to make a particular object. The process of creation can be quite intricate since you may need a specific set of parts to make an item. All it takes is one missing component to affect the process. You may not be able to make the item without it. Therefore, each and every part plays a role in the process.

II. Context

In Psalm 139:13–16, King David went into vivid detail about how he was created. He first proclaimed that the Lord created Him: *For You formed my inward parts.* He stated where the Lord created Him: *You covered me in my mother's womb.* David then praised the Lord for how He created Him: *I will praise you, for I am fearfully and wonderfully made; marvelous are Your works, and that my soul knows very well.* David acknowledged the Lord's presence when he was being created: *My frame was not hidden from You, when I was made in secret, and skillfully wrought in the lowest parts of the earth.* David also hinted at the Lord's omniscience. He said that the Lord already knew Him before He was born: *And in Your book they all were written, the days fashioned for me, when as yet there were none of them.*

III. Main Points

Just as David described how the Lord created him, the same process applies to you as well. Know that the Lord created you. He formed your inward parts. The Lord knew how to make you, and He used the necessary components in order to do so. He used a biological male and a biological female to bring you into existence. While people may credit the mother and father for the procreation of a child, know that it was the Lord who was behind it, for He created all things.

Know that life begins in the womb. *You covered me in my mother's womb.* Life didn't begin when you were born, but it started at conception. The Lord used the womb as a safe haven to grow, mature, and develop you. He designed it with the intention to nurture you until you were ready to come out of it. The Lord also used the womb to shield and protect you. The womb consists of multiple layers of tissue, and these layers help shelter the developing fetus.

Know that you can worship the Lord because He made you. *I will praise You, for I am fearfully and wonderfully made.* In Hebrew, "fearfully" is *yare*, which means "reverence" (Strong's 3372). "Wonderfully" is *palah*, which means "set apart" and "marvelous" (Strong's 6395). So when you were fearfully and wonderfully made by the Lord, He did it in a manner that was with high regard. His creation is well done to the point that it's set apart.

The Lord didn't make you according to the "big-bang" theory, in which everyone came from a rock. He didn't use evolution, in which your ancestors are apes. The Lord designed you solely with His intellect. He made you in His own image, which means He designed you with attributes and features similar to His. Hence, *marvelous are Your works, and that my soul knows very well.* It's marvelous that the Lord intelligently designed and created you. Now you can have a close and personal relationship with Him.

Know that the Lord was present in your creation. *My frame was not hidden from You, when I was made in secret, and skillfully wrought in the lowest parts of the earth. Your eyes saw my substance being yet unformed.* The Lord is known as Jehovah Shammah, which means "the Lord is there," and this includes the process of your creation. He was there when you were conceived, He was there as you were being developed in the womb, and He was there at the time of your birth.

Know that the Lord was omniscient in your creation. *In Your book they all were written, the days fashioned for me, when as yet there were none of them.* The Lord knows all about you. Before you ever came into existence, He knew when you would be conceived. He also knew when you would be born. He knows all that has happened in your life and what will take place in the future. He also knows when you'll die and where you'll spend eternity. What better creator is there than the Lord God of Israel who knows each and every detail about you?

IV. Conclusion

Praise the Lord Jesus Christ, for the gospel was *fearfully and wonderfully made* through Him. It was fearfully made in the sense that the Lord had high regard for all the souls of mankind. He doesn't want a single person to die in their sins and burn in the pit of hell. It was wonderfully made since it paved the only way for man to be reconciled to God. Through the gospel, we can receive God's love, forgiveness, joy, and peace, as well as His amazing grace.

Marvelous are the works of the Lord Jesus Christ. Throughout His ministry, He performed numerous healings and miracles. His most marvelous work was the one done on the cross. It was at the cross that He took on the punishment for all the sins of mankind. Through His marvelous work, your soul can know Him very well and can have a relationship with God. If you have yet to do so, believe on the Lord Jesus Christ. Then your soul can know Him very well and you can receive the gift of everlasting life.

V. Discussion Questions

1. What stood out to you about this lesson and the passages discussed?

2. In the Lord's creation of you, which part means the most to you? Why?

3. In what way can the Lord's creation of you give you a greater appreciation of Him?

4. How does the Lord's view on how you were made differ from the world's view on how you were made?

5. The Lord was there throughout the entire process of your creation. How can this give you a better understanding of Him?

6. Before you were born, the Lord already knew everything about you. How can this give you a better understanding of who He is?

7. Is there anything that you can take away from this discussion and apply to your life? Any final thoughts?

The Word of God

To My Brother in Christ, Mike T.

*For the word of God is living and powerful, and sharper
than any two-edged sword, piercing even to the division
of soul and spirit, and of joints and marrow, and is
a discerner of the thoughts and intents of the heart.*

—Hebrews 4:12

I. Introduction

Think of a time when you had to follow a set of instructions to achieve an intended outcome. Maybe you had a manual on how to assemble a product. Perhaps you used a recipe to help you prepare a meal. Maybe a fitness trainer designed a workout plan to get you in shape. Maybe your GPS gave you directions on how to get to a specific location.

Instructions are given to guide you in the right direction. They tell you what to do and what not to do. In this way, it's easier for you to achieve a desired result. Additionally, it can save you from much heartache and frustration. Trying to figure things out on your own may backfire. The product may not be as functional, the food doesn't taste as good, your level of fitness isn't where you want it to be, or you could get lost in your travels.

II. Context

In Hebrews 4:11–12, the author told the Jewish Christians to follow the instructions of the Lord. If they did so, they wouldn't repeat the same mistakes that their forefathers did in the days of Moses. *Let us therefore be diligent to enter that rest, lest anyone fall according to the same example of disobedience.* He then used the authority of Scripture as one of the reasons why they should be diligent to enter the Lord's rest: *For the word of God is living and powerful, and sharper than any two-edged sword, piercing even to the division of soul and spirit, and of joints and marrow, and is a discerner of the thoughts and intents of the heart.*

III. Main Points

As the author of Hebrews told the Jewish Christians, know that the Word of God *is living and powerful.* God's Word is living because *the word of our God stands forever* (Isaiah 40:8). It has been around for thousands of years. It has also been passed down from generation to generation. His Word survived forty years in the wilderness and multiple rebellions during the time of the judges. It has made it through the wicked kings of Israel and Judah, seventy years of Babylonian captivity, and the rule of the Media-Persian, Grecian, and Roman empires.

The Word of God has lasted through the Middle Ages, when the Inquisition of the Roman Catholic Church kept it out of the hands of the public and executed anyone who dared to distribute it. It's currently the best-selling book of all time, even though governments of numerous countries have banned it. So while opponents of God's Word may attempt to get rid of it, they're all unsuccessful in their efforts. *Heaven and earth will pass away, but My words will by no means pass away* (Matthew 24:35; Luke 21:33). The Word of God is here to stay.

The Word of God is powerful because it saves lives. *Faith comes by hearing, and hearing by the word of God* (Romans 10:17). People who were once *dead in trespasses and sins* (Ephesians 2:1) are now spiritually alive through God's Word. One reason for this is that the true gospel is found in the Word of God. The Old Testament prophecies point to Christ, and the New Testament shows how He fulfilled them. Through the gospel, people have come to believe on the Lord Jesus for their salvation.

The Word of God is *sharper than any two-edged sword. Your word is truth* (John 17:17). It is not subjective, when everyone has his own truth. It is not like Daoism, in which the truth is what feels good to you. Instead, the Word of God is the absolute truth. It informs you on what is right and wrong according to God's standards of perfection. *Through Your precepts I get understanding; therefore I hate every false way* (Psalm 119:104). Through His Word, you can discern the truth from the lies.

The Word of God is *piercing even to the division of soul and spirit, and of joints and marrow*. God's Word leaves no stone unturned. It addresses the overwhelming majority of life's issues. It certainly doesn't hide from the lightning-rod topics of today or the controversial issues of any time period. It doesn't matter what society or the culture believes. If the culture's ideology aligns with the Word of God, then it's right; but if it's in contradiction to God's Word, then it's wrong. His Word is unwavering and will never change for anyone or anything. *Indeed, let God be true but every man a liar* (Romans 3:4).

The Word of God *is a discerner of the thoughts and intents of the heart*. To discern means to screen out and recognize something. The Word of God discerns in that it reveals your true condition. It's like a spiritual X-ray that looks beyond your outward actions and searches the inner motives. It checks out why you do the things you do. Therefore, His Word can spot whether you've done good deeds out of love for the Lord or for ulterior motives, such as selfish gain. So while you can fool man, you can't fool God—nor His Word.

IV. Conclusion

The Word of God is living and powerful because it tells us about the good news of Jesus Christ. It tells us that He is the Word Himself, as well as God: *In the beginning was the Word, and the Word was with God, and the Word was God* (John 1:1). It tells us that He came to save sinners: *I did not come to call the righteous, but sinners, to repentance* (Mark 2:17). It tells us that He came to destroy the works of the devil, who wants to destroy us: *For this purpose the Son of God was manifested, that He might destroy the works of the devil* (1 John 3:8).

The Word of God tells us about Christ's death, burial, and resurrection: *Christ died for our sins according to the Scriptures, and . . . He was buried, and . . . He rose again the third day according to the Scriptures* (1 Corinthians 15:3–4). It tells us that He died for the sins of the whole world: *He Himself is the propitiation for our sins, and not for ours only but also for the whole world* (1 John 2:2). It tells us how we can receive a saving faith: *If you confess with your mouth the Lord Jesus and believe in your heart that God has raised Him from the dead, you will be saved* (Romans 10:9). If you have not yet done so, *repent, and believe in the gospel* (Mark 1:15). By doing so, you can be saved from eternal fire and have the gift of everlasting life.

V. Discussion Questions

1. What stood out to you about this lesson and the passages discussed?

2. When you think of the Word of God, what comes to mind?

3. How is the Word of God *living*?

4. How is the Word of God *powerful*?

5. How is the Word of God *sharper than any two-edged sword, piercing even to the division of the soul and spirit, and of joints and marrow*?

6. How is the Word of God *a discerner of the thoughts and intents of the heart*?

7. Is there anything that you can take away from this discussion and apply to your life? Any final thoughts?

Lesson 29

In the Secret Place of the Most High

To My Sister in Christ, Ms. Barbara (George's Mom)

He who dwells in the secret place
of the Most High
shall abide under the
shadow of the Almighty.

—Psalm 91:1

I. Introduction

Think of something that keeps you from further harm. Someone may get insurance to financially cover themselves in case disaster strikes. Beachgoers tend to put on sunscreen to protect their skin from ultraviolet (UV) rays. The majority of people will put on extra layers of clothing in freezing weather to prevent frostbite. Campers may coat themselves in bug spray to shield themselves from mosquito bites.

These are all forms of protection. Protection is something you use to keep yourself from harm. You may seek protection because it's human nature to keep away from harm. *A prudent man foresees evil and hides himself, but the simple pass on and are punished* (Proverbs 22:3). It's not a bad thing to protect yourself from potential danger, and in the majority of cases, it's considered wise. However, the issue is where you go for protection and how much trust you place in it. Placing too much trust in something can lead you astray. It can cause you to not go to the Lord as the main source of your protection.

II. Context

In Psalm 91, the author went into vivid detail about the Lord's protection for believers. He began the psalm with the legitimacy of the Lord's protection: *He who dwells in the secret place of the Most High shall abide under the shadow of the Almighty.* The secret place is a reference to *His tabernacle* (Psalm 27:5). The tabernacle was an earthly dwelling place for the Lord in the Old Testament. So *he who dwells in the secret place of the Most High* is the one who is in the presence of the Lord and is under His protection. The psalmist also stated why he put his trust in the Lord: *He is my refuge and my fortress; my God, in Him I will trust* (Psalm 91:2). Throughout the rest of the psalm, he explained how the Lord protects those who put their trust in Him.

III. Main Points

The Lord protects you through His provision. *Surely He shall deliver you from the snare of the fowler and from the perilous pestilence* (Psalm 91:3). The Lord is gracious since He can give you enough of His strength to persevere in difficult seasons. Whether He arms you with His peace, joy, or longsuffering, there is always hope with the Lord. Because there is hope, you can press on. He is able to shield you from the darkness of absolute despair and show you the light at the end of the tunnel.

He protects you with His truth. *His truth shall be your shield and buckler* (Psalm 91:4). The Lord uses the truth of His ways, as well as His Word, to guide you in all areas of your life. Given that *every word of God is pure* (Proverbs 30:5), He will inform you of what's right and wrong. With knowledge of right and wrong, He can give you discernment. With discernment, you're able to recognize the truth of God and protect yourself from the lies of the devil. Hence, you don't need to fear, even if trouble heads your way. *You shall not be afraid of the terror by night, nor of the arrow that flies by day* (Psalm 91:5).

The Lord protects you through His omnipotence. *A thousand may fall at your side, and ten thousand at your right hand; but it shall not come near you* (Psalm 91:7). The demonic attacks that come from Satan and the fallen angels are not to be taken lightly. They have caused many, if not all of us, to stumble at one point or another. Satan tends to go for your weaknesses, and he *transforms himself into an angel of light* (2 Corinthians 11:14) so that you may be deceived by him. However, *He who is in you is greater than he who is in the world* (1 John 4:4). The Holy Spirit is more powerful than your adversaries because He is God. God is omnipotent, which means He is all-powerful. He can protect you against spiritual attacks and shield you from the demonic forces of the world.

The Lord protects you through His promises. *Because you have made the Lord, who is my refuge, even the Most High, your dwelling place, no evil shall befall you, nor shall any plague come near your dwelling* (Psalm 91:9–10). The Lord promises to protect those who put their trust in Him. *Whoever trusts in the Lord shall be safe* (Proverbs 29:25). This doesn't mean that the Lord will keep you away from all hardship, but it does mean that He will preserve and strengthen you in the spiritual realm. He will keep you spiritually intact if you go to Him as your source of refuge and strength.

The Lord protects you with His angels. *For He shall give His angels charge over you, to keep you in all your ways* (Psalm 91:11). Whether you realize it or not, there is spiritual warfare that takes place before you. While Satan uses his demons to wreak havoc in your life, the Lord sends His angels to counter them. *In their hands they shall bear you up, lest you dash your foot against a stone* (Psalm 91:12). He even assigned an angel to look after an entire country. Michael the archangel looks after the nation of Israel. He is *the great prince who stands watch over the sons of [Daniel's] people* (Daniel 12:1).

The Lord protects those who love Him. *Because he has set his love upon Me, therefore I will deliver him; I will set him on high, because he has known My name* (Psalm 91:14). God is pleased when we love Him because loving Him is an act of obedience. To love the Lord is to obey the first and great commandment: *Love the Lord your God with all your heart, with all your soul, and with all your mind* (Matthew 22:37). If you're obedient to the Lord, He is more likely to bless you spiritually. God says, *Those who honor Me I will honor* (1 Samuel 2:30).

IV. Conclusion

The Lord is the only one who can protect you from the eternal consequences of sin and death. He provided a way out of the pit of hell and the lake of fire through His Son, Jesus Christ. The Lord Jesus is the source of protection because He took upon Himself the sins of the whole world. *He was wounded for our transgressions, He was bruised for our iniquities; the chastisement for our peace was upon Him, and by His stripes we are healed* (Isaiah 53:5).

Through Jesus, the second death has no power over you. Through Jesus, there will come a day when you will be protected from all pain and suffering. *God will wipe away every tear from their eyes; there shall be no more death, nor sorrow, nor crying. There shall be no more pain, for the former things have passed away* (Revelation 21:4). If you have not yet done so, repent and put your trust in the Lord Jesus. *With long life I will satisfy him, and show him My salvation* (Psalm 91:16). If you believe in Him, He will satisfy you with everlasting life and will deliver you from hellfire.

V. Discussion Questions

1. What stood out to you about this lesson and the passages discussed?

2. When you think of the Lord's protection, what comes to mind?

3. Of the different ways the Lord can protect you, which way sticks out to you the most? Why?

4. What are some ways the Lord has protected you?

5. How can the Lord's protection help you put your trust in Him?

6. What does the Lord's protection teach you in regard to His character? How can it give you a better understanding of who He is?

7. Is there anything that you can take away from this discussion and apply to your life? Any final thoughts?

Swift to Hear, Slow to Speak, Slow to Wrath

Dedicated to Peter (Market Street Mission)

*So then, my beloved brethren, let every man be
swift to hear, slow to speak, slow to wrath.*

—James 1:19

I. Introduction

Can you recall a time when you were told something that benefited you? For instance, maybe your parents or guardians told you not to touch the hot stove. Perhaps your teacher informed you to study for the exam next week or your boss gave you feedback on how to do your job better. Your doctor may have instructed you on how to recover from an injury or illness.

These examples show the different scenarios in which one listens to the advising party. When you listen, you hear someone out. You pay attention and set your focus on what someone has to say. Then you receive the details of the speaking party. You process what was said. Then you decide what you will do with the information.

II. Context

In James 1:19–20, James issued a set of exhortations to the Jewish Christians. He believed that because the Lord saved them through His Word, they should listen to it as well: *So then my beloved brethren, let every man be swift to hear.* James then gave the brethren a second exhortation to help them with the first one: *slow to speak.* James afterward provided a third exhortation and the reason behind it: *slow to wrath; for the wrath of man does not produce the righteousness of God.*

III. Main Points

As James informed his Jewish brethren, *be swift to hear.* Be swift and quick to hear God's Word because His *word is truth* (John 17:17). The truth may not be easy to follow, but it will always lead you in the right direction. *Your word is a lamp to my feet and a light to my path* (Psalm 119:105). It will guide you through the blackness and darkness of this world, as well as bring you to where the Lord wants you to be.

Be swift to hear God's Word because it can help you worship Him *in spirit and truth* (John 4:24). You're placed here on earth to serve and worship the Lord, but it helps to know about the Lord and why you should worship Him. In this way, you can properly do so. Through the Word of God, you can gain a better understanding of Him and His character. *Knowledge of the Holy One is understanding* (Proverbs 9:10). The more you increase your knowledge of the Lord, the more you can appreciate Him. The more you appreciate Him, the more you may want to worship Him and the more you may want the Holy Spirit to guide you and help you worship the Lord in a way that is acceptable to Him.

Be *slow to speak.* Be slow to speak because you can lead others astray with your words. If you're not careful, you can rush to judgment and speak about something you don't know much about. You may fail to adequately research to see whether or not the content you want to share is factual, as well as biblical. As a result, you can spread misinformation, lies, and heresies to other people. It may seem like it is not a big deal if you spread misinformation to only a few people, but that misinformation can spread like a virus. The people you told may tell others, and the people they told may tell others, and so on. *A little leaven leavens the whole lump* (Galatians 5:9). The misinformation you share could be a stumbling block to others and lead them in the wrong direction.

Be *slow to speak* because *death and life are in the power of the tongue* (Proverbs 18:21). With the words you speak, you can lift someone up and bring life into them. The reverse is also true. With your words, you can tear someone down and destroy them. Therefore, be very careful with what you say to other people because you're to edify those around you and not be a hindrance to them. Also, you will have to give an account to God for the words you speak. *Every idle word men may speak, they will give account of it in the day of judgment. For by your words you will be justified, and by your words you will be condemned* (Matthew 12:36–37).

Be *slow to wrath; for the wrath of man does not produce the righteousness of God.* Outbursts of anger are a work of the flesh and are sinful in the sight of God. When you're quick to explode on someone, bad fruit is produced. You can scar someone to the point where they have mental, emotional, and psychological trauma. You can also damage your relationship with that person in such a way that they may not want to be around you. You may gain a reputation as a reviler so that people will start to distance themselves from you and your rage. Moreover, you become a poor reflection of Christ and bring shame to His name. Keep in mind the importance of self-control. *He who is slow to anger is better than the mighty, and he who rules his spirit than he who takes a city* (Proverbs 16:32).

IV. Conclusion

The Lord Jesus Christ was *swift to hear.* Throughout His ministry on earth, Jesus heard and listened to the questions, as well as to the comments, of the people. He listened to numerous healing requests. He listened to the various questions from the disciples, such as those about His second coming and the purpose of His parables. He listened to the questions from the Pharisees that they asked to try to trap Him.

Jesus was *slow to speak.* Jesus wasn't quick to respond when the chief priests, scribes, and false witnesses accused Him of blasphemy. *He was oppressed and He was afflicted, yet He opened not His mouth; He was led as a lamb to the slaughter, and as a sheep before its shearers is silent, so He opened not His mouth* (Isaiah 53:7).

Jesus was *slow to wrath.* If Jesus had wanted to, He could have wiped out the Pharisees with twelve legions (seventy-two thousand) of angels. The Lord could also have wiped all of us out due to our sin. However, the Lord *is longsuffering toward us, not willing that any should perish but that all should come to repentance* (2 Peter 3:9). This includes you. If you have not yet done so, *repent, and believe in the gospel* (Mark 1:15). If you do, God will be swift to forgive you and will establish an everlasting relationship with you.

V. Discussion Questions

1. What stood out to you about this lesson and the passages discussed?

2. In the exhortation to *be swift to hear, slow to speak, slow to wrath,* which one sticks out to you the most? Why?

3. In what ways can it be tempting to be slow to hear, swift to speak, and swift to wrath?

4. In what ways can you be *swift to hear*?

5. How can you be *slow to speak*?

6. How can you be *slow to wrath*?

7. Is there anything that you can take away from this discussion and apply to your life? Any final thoughts?

Keep Your Heart

To My Brother in Christ, Ryan H.

Keep your heart with all diligence, for out of it spring the issues of life.

—Proverbs 4:23

I. Introduction

Think of a time when you had to protect something that was really valuable to you. For example, maybe you put your savings into a bank account, got a home security system for your house, or purchased virus protection for your computer. Maybe you have health, car, home, and life insurance. Perhaps you have identity theft protection to guard yourself against identity theft.

These are all ways to protect yourself. To protect means to shield or keep something from harm. The object of protection is usually something of value. Because it's something of value, you guard it from danger. Defending the item of value from potential threats reduces the chances of a successful attack against it. It lowers the possibility of it being stolen, damaged, or destroyed. Also, protecting something you value saves you from the pain and sorrow that you would feel if you were to lose it.

II. Context

In Proverbs 4:23, Solomon issued advice concerning the heart. He first provided an exhortation. He urged his audience to guard and protect their hearts. Not only did he tell them to protect their hearts, but he told them to protect it with all determination and effort. *Keep your heart with all diligence.* Solomon then provided a reason why they should guard their hearts. He recognized that it can be the source of many problems: *for out of it spring the issues of life.*

III. Main Points

As Solomon told his audience, *keep your heart.* To keep means to guard and protect. "Heart" is *leb* in Hebrew, which means the center of something (Strong's 3820). To keep your heart means to protect the center of yourself, which is your innermost being. Your innermost being contains your character, which consists of the set of qualities that you possess. Therefore, to keep your heart may also mean to defend yourself against negative influences that harm your character.

Keep your heart with all diligence. Diligence is synonymous with attentiveness, consistency, and effort. To *keep your heart with all diligence* means to pay attention to how you guard it. The way you protect yourself plays a part in your ability to do so. One way you can keep your heart is through prevention. *A prudent man foresees evil and hides himself, but the simple pass on and are punished* (Proverbs 22:3). If you remove yourself from the element of harm, then the chances that you will encounter it will likely decrease. It's more difficult for bad influences to reach you if you don't let them.

What if you can't remove yourself from a toxic environment? *Pray without ceasing* (1 Thessalonians 5:17). Regardless of the situation, you're to go to the Lord in faith because He will provide for your needs. You're to seek wisdom from Him since He will lead you into all truth. With the Lord's wisdom, you can discern whether to have patience with a difficult person or confront them in love. In extreme cases, you may have to contact the authorities to intervene and confront the individual. Nevertheless, the Lord can give you His peace in tough situations, and it is the peace of God that *will guard your hearts and minds through Christ Jesus* (Philippians 4:7).

Another way you can keep your heart is through godly counsel. *In the multitude of counselors there is safety* (Proverbs 11:14). There is safety in the presence of godly counsel because you can be immersed in sound wisdom and advice. Godly people can remind you of biblical truths. Their holy lifestyle can be used as an example and blueprint of how to apply God's Word in your life. Hence, *he who walks with wise men will be wise* (Proverbs 13:20).

Keep your heart with all diligence, for out of it spring the issues of life. Outward actions are a good indicator of what's in your heart because your actions reflect the heart's condition. *A good man out of the good treasure of his heart brings forth good; and an evil man out of the evil treasure of his heart brings forth evil. For out of the abundance of the heart his mouth speaks* (Luke 6:45).

If your heart is corrupted by negative influences and sin, it can defile your character. You can acquire traits that contradict the Word of God and resemble the works of the flesh. The negative traits can manifest in bad behavior. Bad behavior leads to undesirable consequences. The issues of life spring from the heart because your behavior stems from the condition of your heart, and your conduct leads to different outcomes, whether good or bad.

IV. Conclusion

Keep your heart with all diligence through the gospel of Jesus Christ. Remember that our hearts are not good. *The heart is deceitful above all things, and desperately wicked; who can know it?* (Jeremiah 17:9). Because our hearts are wicked, they will lead us into sin. Our sin will bring forth disastrous results in our lives. *Sin, when it is full-grown, brings forth death* (James 1:15).

Jesus tells us to go to Him, for He is *gentle and lowly in heart* (Matthew 11:29). He is of a gentle and humble character. He is gentle in that He has compassion toward us. He doesn't want us to die in our sins and burn in everlasting fire. He is humble because although He was God, He still sacrificed His life for us. *He humbled Himself and became obedient to the point of death, even the death of the cross* (Philippians 2:8). Because of this, He can give a new heart to anyone who believes on Him. *I will give you a new heart and put a new spirit within you; I will take the heart of stone out of your flesh and give you a heart of flesh* (Ezekiel 36:26). If you have not yet done so, repent of your sins and believe on the Lord Jesus Christ for salvation. He will give you a new heart and will issue you the gift of everlasting life.

V. Discussion Questions

1. What stood out to you about this lesson and the passages discussed?

2. When you think of "keep your heart," what comes to mind?

3. What does "with all diligence" indicate? Why?

4. In what ways can you *keep your heart with all diligence?*

5. How does the heart spring forth *the issues of life?*

6. How can this verse point you toward your need for God?

7. Is there anything that you can take away from this discussion and apply to your life? Any final thoughts?

Lesson 32

A Broken Heart

To My Sister in Christ, Marie C.

The Lord is near to those who have a broken heart,
and saves such as have a contrite spirit.

—Psalm 34:18

I. Introduction

Have you ever been in a really low spot and wondered if anybody cared? Maybe you got bullied at school and nobody seemed to notice. Perhaps you were in an abusive relationship and not a single person was concerned. Maybe you suffer from depression, and the only one who knows about it is you. Perhaps you were stranded in the middle of a storm and help was nowhere in sight.

If you've been in such a predicament, you may find it difficult to believe that people care about you. One reason people care is because of empathy. Empathy is when you have the ability to understand and share the feelings of another. You have compassion for someone who is in a tough position. You feel sorrow toward them and hope their circumstances improve. There's a good chance that you'll pray for them. You may even intervene through financial support or another type of aid.

II. Context

In Psalm 34:17–18, David talked about the Lord's sympathy and intervention for those who are in trouble. He informed his readers that the Lord hears the righteous when they are in trouble: *The righteous cry out, and the Lord hears.* He also stated that the Lord will take action on their behalf: *He delivers them out of all their troubles.* David noted the Lord's proximity to those who are down: *The Lord is near to those who have a broken heart.* David then stated an additional promise of the Lord: *[He] saves such as have a contrite spirit.*

III. Main Points

Similarly to what David told his audience, know that *the righteous cry out, and the Lord hears.* It is no surprise that Christians find themselves in difficult situations. *All who desire to live godly in Christ Jesus will suffer persecution* (2 Timothy 3:12). Although it is expected that Christians will suffer hardship, it doesn't mean you must stay silent. You can call out to God for help. You can send Him your prayers and supplications.

Remember that *if we ask anything according to His will, He hears us* (1 John 5:14). It is the Lord's desire to provide you with everything you need. If you ask Him for help, and your request aligns with His desires for you, He will listen. He will provide you with what you need. It may not be what you want, but it will be what you need. What He provides will be far greater than what you could do on your own. *Let us therefore come boldly to the throne of grace, that we may obtain mercy and find grace to help in time of need* (Hebrews 4:16).

The Lord *delivers them out of all their troubles.* To deliver means to provide, assist, and rescue. The Lord does all three for the righteous. He provides whatever is necessary for you to make it through a difficult season. He assists and guides you in the way you should go. He can use godly people to direct you, His Word to instruct you, or circumstances to reveal His will for you. The Lord rescues you by either removing you from hardship or giving you the strength to endure it.

The Lord is near to those who have a broken heart. A broken heart is usually accompanied by sadness and sorrow. A broken heart usually stems from a tragic event or a series of calamities. You may be filled with mourning and weeping due to the trauma, but *blessed are those who mourn, for they shall be comforted* (Matthew 5:4). The Lord is in close proximity to those who weep and are in sorrow. So if you're in distress, He can console you with the presence of His Spirit and the promises of His Word. God is a *God of all comfort, who comforts us in all our tribulation* (2 Corinthians 1:3–4).

The Lord *saves such as have a contrite spirit.* "Contrite" is *dakka'* in Hebrew, which means "crushed" or "destruction" (Strong's 1793). When you have a contrite spirit, you are crushed and destroyed from within. It's as if the wind has been taken from your sails and you lose motivation to press forward in life. It seems as if there's no light at the end of the tunnel.

However, when there seems to be no light at the end of the tunnel, the Lord tends to intervene and shine. When you are weak, then you are strong (2 Corinthians 12:10). When you lose the will to press on, the Lord is able to save you from yourself and give you the strength to persevere. Therefore, *blessed are the poor in spirit, for theirs is the kingdom of heaven* (Matthew 5:3). You are fortunate and well off if you're down in spirit because the Lord can revive you and work in you for His glory.

IV. Conclusion

[The Lord Jesus Christ] is near to those who have a broken heart over their sins. He is near to those who have godly sorrow over their wicked acts against Him. G*odly sorrow produces repentance leading to salvation, not to be regretted* (2 Corinthians 7:10). The Lord Jesus *saves such as have a contrite spirit.* He came to save those who feel crushed due to their sin and are in need of a Savior. Remember that *the sacrifices of God are a broken spirit, a broken and a contrite heart—these, O God, You will not despise* (Psalm 51:17).

If you have not yet done so, cry out to the Lord Jesus Christ for your salvation. *The righteous cry out, and the* LORD *hears, and delivers them out of all their troubles* (Psalm 34:17). If you cry out to Jesus for salvation, He will deliver you from the troubles of eternal torment in hell and the lake of fire. *For whoever shall call on the name of the Lord shall be saved* (Joel 2:32; Acts 2:21; Romans 10:13).

V. Discussion Questions

1. What stood out to you about this lesson and the passages discussed?

2. If *the righteous cry out,* how should you deal with difficult situations?

3. *The righteous cry out, and the Lord hears.* How can this give you a better appreciation of the Lord?

4. Can you recall a time when the Lord delivered you out of all your troubles? Can you give an example from Scripture when the Lord delivered someone out of all his or her troubles?

5. Can you recall a time when you had a broken heart and the Lord was near to you?

6. He *saves such as have a contrite spirit.* How can this give you hope in difficult situations?

7. Is there anything that you can take away from this discussion and apply to your life? Any final thoughts?

Lesson 33

A Living Sacrifice

To My Brother in Christ, Chris John B.

I beseech you therefore, brethren, by the mercies of God,
that you present your bodies a living sacrifice, holy,
acceptable to God, which is your reasonable service.

—Romans 12:1

I. Introduction

Think of a situation in which you gave something up. For example, maybe you handed money to the cashier so you could purchase a product and complete the transaction. Perhaps you quit smoking to protect yourself from lung disease, or you refrained from junk food to lose weight and get in shape. Maybe you cut down on social media and television so you could focus on your studies.

These are examples of sacrifice. To sacrifice means to lay something down or give it up. What you surrender is typically something you value. It may give you some sort of pleasure, comfort, or security. However, you also realize that if you hold on to your possession or continue in a certain pattern, the cons outweigh the benefits. Therefore, you sacrifice it because the long-term gain is greater than any short-term pain.

II. Context

In Romans 12:1, the apostle Paul made an exhortation to the Romans based upon the closing statement of the previous chapter. He believed that all things are of the

Lord, and therefore all glory goes solely to Him. Based upon this revelation, Paul urged the Romans to sacrifice themselves before the Lord: *I beseech you therefore, brethren, by the mercies of God, that you present your bodies a living sacrifice.* Paul then told his audience how to follow his exhortation: *holy, acceptable to God.* Next he reminded the Romans that it was their duty to conduct themselves in such a manner: *which is your reasonable service.*

III. Main Points

What Paul told the Romans is relevant to you: *I beseech you therefore, brethren, by the mercies of God.* "Beseech" means to urge or plead with someone. You really want someone to do something. Mercy is when you don't get what you deserve. You may have done something wrong, but the offended party decides to spare you from punishment.

One example of God's mercy is with mankind. You and all people have sinned before God, as well as broken His commandments. *The wages of sin is death* (Romans 6:23). This means that everyone deserves to die because of their sin. However, the Lord doesn't want anyone to die in their sin. His desire is for everyone to believe on His Son, Jesus Christ, for salvation so they don't have to face His wrath.

Another example of God's mercy can be found in the previous chapter, Romans 11. The nation of Israel rejected Jesus as their Messiah. God could have cut them off from being His chosen nation, but *God has not cast away His people whom He foreknew* (Romans 11:2). God foreknew Israel in the sense that He already acknowledged them as His physical nation, even before the world began. So despite their rejection, the Lord isn't done with them. Jesus will come back for Israel when He returns to the earth.

Through God's mercy, you can have the opportunity to *present your bodies a living sacrifice.* To present means to show or offer. The body can represent life here on earth. You live in your body, and you can't complete a single action without it. So when you present your body as a living sacrifice, you surrender your lifestyle. You give up the right to live for yourself. You no longer appease your flesh and do whatever you want to do. Instead, you dedicate your life to a cause other than yourself. You live your life in honor of that cause.

Present your bodies a living sacrifice, holy, acceptable to God. If you present your body as a living sacrifice to the Lord, you do what He wants you to do. In the Old Testament, the Levitical priests followed certain guidelines in order to offer an acceptable sacrifice to the Lord. They had to follow the instructions of the Lord. If they failed to adhere to His protocols, the sacrifice would be rejected. In some cases, the Lord killed those who offered bad sacrifices. Their sacrifices were so abominable that He struck them dead (e.g., Leviticus 10:1–2).

Likewise, there is a way that the Lord wants you to live. He wants you to live in holiness. "Holy" is *hagios* in Greek, which means that no one can rightly accuse you of any fault (Strong's 40). Your motives also become pure, which means you do the right things for the right reasons. Holiness is acceptable to God because it represents who He is. The Lord is El Hakkadosh: the Holy God. He is blameless, pure, and perfect in every way. Therefore, *be holy, for I am holy* (Leviticus 11:44; 1 Peter 1:16).

Also remember that it is *your reasonable service* to present your body a living sacrifice to the Lord. It should be your mission to dedicate your life to the Lord and live in a way that's pleasing to Him. By doing so, you can show your appreciation for Him. Remember that *we love Him because he first loved us* (1 John 4:19). If He literally laid down His life for you, then why can't you figuratively do the same for Him? It is fair and just to give yourself up to the One who gave Himself up for you.

IV. Conclusion

The Lord Jesus presented His body a living sacrifice, holy and acceptable to God the Father. Jesus's sacrifice on the cross was holy in that He was set apart. He lived a perfect life without sin. Therefore, His sacrifice was acceptable to God and was able to atone for the sins of the whole world. It was Jesus's reasonable service to sacrifice His body because He came to the earth to destroy Satan through His death. *Inasmuch then as the children have partaken of flesh and blood, He Himself likewise shared in the same, that through death He might destroy him who had the power of death, that is, the devil* (Hebrews 2:14).

It was Jesus's reasonable service to sacrifice His body because God the Father sent Him to earth to provide salvation for us. *He made Him who knew no sin to be sin for us, that we might become the righteousness of God in Him* (2 Corinthians 5:21). If you have not yet done so, *present your bodies a living sacrifice, holy, acceptable to God.* Surrender your life to the Lord Jesus and believe on Him today. *Believe on the Lord Jesus Christ, and you will be saved* (Acts 16:31).

V. Discussion Questions

1. What stood out to you about this lesson and the passages discussed?

2. When you think of "present your bodies a living sacrifice," what comes to mind?

3. How can *the mercies of God* help you *present your bodies a living sacrifice?*

4. What are some ways you can *present your bodies a living sacrifice, holy, acceptable to God?*

5. How can it be challenging to *present your bodies a living sacrifice, holy, acceptable to God?*

6. How is it *your reasonable service* to *present your bodies a living sacrifice, holy, acceptable to God?*

7. Is there anything that you can take away from this discussion and apply to your life? Any final thoughts?

Lesson 34

The Renewing of Your Mind

To My Brother in Christ, Chris John B. #2

And do not be conformed to this world, but be transformed by the renewing of your mind, that you may prove what is that good and acceptable and perfect will of God.

—Romans 12:2

I. Introduction

Have you ever witnessed something change into something else? Take the life cycle of butterflies as an example. They roam around as caterpillars for about two to five weeks before they go into a cocoon. After one or two weeks, they emerge from the cocoon as fully developed butterflies.[1] Body composition is another example. A man can enter the weight room with a slim physique, but if he consistently puts in the work, he may develop a muscular frame.

If the answer is yes, then you have witnessed the process of transformation. The prefix "trans" means across from one place to another. It can also mean a change. "Form" can be defined as the configuration of something or the particular way something exists. So "transform" means to change in composition and configuration. It's to alter the way something exists, to go across from one state to another.

---

1   "Life Cyle of a Butterfly: Amazing!" Joyful Butterfly, April 23, 2014, https://www.joyfulbutterfly.com/life-cycle-of-a-butterfly/.

II. Context

In Romans 12:2, the apostle Paul issued a warning and an exhortation to the Romans. He first told them what not to do: *And do not be conformed to this world.* He then told them what they should do: *but be transformed by the renewing of your mind.* Following the warning and exhortation, he provided a reason why they should follow his instructions: *that you may prove what is that good and acceptable and perfect will of God.*

III. Main Points

As Paul warned the Romans, *do not be conformed to this world.* To conform means to adapt in a way in which you are similar or akin to something. If you're a Christian, you're in this world, but not of the world. You may live on the same planet as everyone else, but you shouldn't adapt to the ways of the world and have similar lifestyles as the people of this world. One reason is that the world indulges in sin. If you live similarly to the world, there's a good chance you'll partake in sin. Remember that *he who sins is of the devil* (1 John 3:8). Therefore, if you conform to the world, your lifestyle will reflect that of an unbeliever, which will be a poor testimony to those around you.

If you conform to the world, you displease the Lord. *Whoever therefore wants to be a friend of the world makes himself an enemy of God* (James 4:4). You oppose God and what He stands for. One reason conformity to the world displeases God is because you can't have it both ways. You can't call yourself a Christian and live like a non-Christian. If the world partakes in an activity that the Bible calls a sin, then you abstain from it. If you try to play both sides, it's hypocrisy, which is something God detests. Hence, *if anyone loves the world, the love of the Father is not in him* (1 John 2:15).

Instead, *be transformed by the renewing of your mind.* When one is transformed by Christ, they are changed into a new creation. *Therefore, if anyone is in Christ, he is a new creation; old things are passed away; behold, all things have become new* (2 Corinthians 5:17). You don't stay where you're at, but you continue to grow and mature in the faith.

"Renewing" is *anakainósis* in Greek, which means "renovation" (Strong's 342). You repair something that was in subpar condition and make it good again. When you renew your mind, you update it with new information. The updated information could lead to a change in mindset and perspective. *For to be carnally minded is*

144

death, but to be spiritually minded is life and peace (Romans 8:6). When your mind is renewed, the filth and lies of the world are removed. Your mind is purified and sanctified by the truth of God's Word. Therefore, you can set your mind on the way of righteousness, as well as on holiness.

Be transformed by the renewing of your mind, that you may prove what is that good and acceptable and perfect will of God (Romans 12:2). *Through Your precepts I get understanding; therefore I hate every false way* (Psalm 119:104). Setting your mind on the Lord and growing in faith will usually lead to an increase in holiness. It can lead to a growth in godly attributes, such as *love, joy, peace, longsuffering, kindness, goodness, faithfulness, gentleness, [and] self-control* (Galatians 5:22–23).

Godly attributes show *what is that good and acceptable and perfect will of God.* They show what is *good* since all good things come from the Lord. *Every good gift and every perfect gift is from above, and comes down from the Father of lights, with whom there is no variation or shadow of turning* (James 1:17). Godly attributes are *acceptable* since they don't violate Scripture. *Against such there is no law* (Galatians 5:23).

Godly attributes represent the *perfect will of God* since they bring Him glory. *We are His workmanship, created in Christ Jesus for good works, which God prepared beforehand that we should walk in them* (Ephesians 2:10). God has designed you to walk in righteousness, and His desire is for you to bring glory to Him. If you follow God and walk in righteousness, you do His will because obedience is a way to worship Him. *If you love Me, keep My commandments* (John 14:15). Godly attributes can also lead others to glorify God because they will be able to see the Lord's character and can praise Him for His magnificence. Therefore, *let your light so shine before men, that they may see your good works and glorify your Father in heaven* (Matthew 5:16).

IV. Conclusion

Jesus did not conform to this world. He may have been in the world, but He was not of the world. He may have eaten with sinners and tax collectors, but He didn't conform to their lifestyles. Instead, He challenged people to *be transformed by the renewing of [their] mind[s]* through repentance. For example, after John the Baptist was put in prison, Jesus proclaimed, *Repent, for the kingdom of heaven is at hand* (Matthew 4:17). After He had forgiven the woman caught in adultery, He told her, *Go and sin no more* (John 8:11). When a group of people told Jesus that Pilate had executed some Galileans, He told them, *Unless you repent you will all likewise perish* (Luke 13:3).

Jesus wants us to renew our minds through repentance as well. He wants us to change our minds about sin and turn away from it. He *now commands all men everywhere to repent* (Acts 17:30). By doing so, we *may prove what is that good and acceptable and perfect will of God.* God's will and desire is for everyone to have an everlasting relationship with Him through His Son. So if you have yet to do so, repent and believe on the Lord Jesus Christ for your salvation—and then you can do the perfect will of God and have everlasting life. *He who does the will of God abides forever* (1 John 2:17).

V. Discussion Questions

1. What stood out to you about this lesson and the passages discussed?

2. How can it be difficult to *not be conformed to this world?*

3. What are some consequences if you are *conformed to this world?*

4. When you think of being transformed by the renewing of your mind, what comes to mind?

5. What are some ways you can *be transformed by the renewing of your mind?*

6. How can the renewing of your mind help you *prove what is that good and acceptable and perfect will of God?*

7. Is there anything that you can take away from this discussion and apply to your life? Any final thoughts?

Lesson 35

God, Who Made the World

To My Sister in Christ, Jackie H.

God, who made the world and everything in it, since He is Lord of heaven and earth, does not dwell in temples made with hands.

—Acts 17:24

I. Introduction

Has there been a situation in which you had to explain the differences between two or more objects? For instance, maybe you noted the distinctions between baking powder and baking soda. Perhaps you described the dissimilarities among the types of running shoes. Maybe you told someone the variances between an all-wheel drive and a four-wheel drive vehicle. It's possible you listed the differences among different job sectors.

These are examples of contrast. When you contrast something, you note the differences between two or more entities. First you do an analysis of each object and assess their qualities and characteristics. Then you make a comparison between the objects. When you compare the objects, you're able to notice and contrast what makes them separate from each other.

II. Context

In Acts 17:24–25, the apostle Paul contrasted the one true God from the other objects that the Athenians worshiped. Paul began his proclamation by mentioning qualities that separated the one true God from all the other false gods. Paul talked about the Lord's creation: *God, who made the world and everything in it*. He also brought up the Lord's dominion: *since He is Lord of heaven and earth*. Paul then mentioned the Lord's location: He *does not dwell in temples made with hands*. Paul continued with how God is worshiped: *Nor is He worshiped with men's hands*. He told that the Lord is self-sustaining: *as though He needed anything*; and he stated the reason why: *since He gives to all life, breath, and all things*.

III. Main Points

Just as Paul told the Athenians, remember that it is God *who made the world and everything in it*. The God of Abraham, Isaac, and Jacob is different from all the other gods because He is the creator of the universe. *In the beginning God created the heavens and the earth* (Genesis 1:1). Within six days, the Lord created the world. He made the heavens, earth, waters, light, day, and night. He also made the firmament, grass, herbs, seeds, trees, and fruit. Additionally, He created the sun, moon, stars, sea creatures, birds, land animals—and man in His own image.

God *is Lord of heaven and earth*. A lord is a ruler and owner. A lord has power, authority, and control over something. When you make something that's new, you tend to have exclusive rights over it. You claim the object as yours because you were the original designer of it. You put in the time, effort, resources, and intellect to make it. Hence, you get credited as its owner.

Because it is *God, who made the world and everything in it*, then *He is Lord of heaven and earth*. He has dominion over the world and possesses an everlasting patent, and nobody else can claim ownership but Him. *In His hand are the deep places of the earth; the heights of the hills are His also. The sea is His, for He made it; and His hands formed the dry land* (Psalm 95:4–5).

God *does not dwell in temples made with hands*. Because God made the world and has dominion over it, He is not confined to a single location. Some gods are at a single location or place, but the Lord God of Israel is omnipresent—He is everywhere at all times. *"Do I not fill heaven and earth?" says the Lord* (Jeremiah 23:24). God resides in the third heaven. His Spirit also dwells on the earth, and He hovers *over the face of the waters* (Genesis 1:2).

God isn't *worshiped with men's hands*. Throughout history, man has worshiped idols via statues and shrines. Whether it was the golden calf in the wilderness, the image of Baal, or Dagon of the Philistines, man created statues of false deities with their hands. However, the God of Israel isn't worshiped with a statue. To do so gives the impression that we created Him. This is completely heretical, for He created us.

God isn't *worshiped with men's hands* because no statue can resemble Him. Nothing can match His glory and majesty. *The idols of the nations are silver and gold, the work of men's hands. They have mouths, but they do not speak; eyes they have, but they do not see; they have ears, but they do not hear; nor is there any breath in their mouths* (Psalm 135:15–17).

God also wants you to worship Him in a specific way. You are to worship Him *in spirit and truth* (John 4:24). You are to adhere to the Holy Spirit since *He will guide you into all truth* (John 16:13). You are to walk in obedience to the truth of God and His Word. Obedience is a form of worship since you can show your love for God through it. *If you love Me, keep My commandments* (John 14:15).

God is in need of nothing: *as though He needed anything.* God doesn't need you to make statues of Him. He desires to have a relationship with you, but He doesn't need you or anyone else to be reconciled to Him. There is nothing that God needs from you because He has everything He needs. The Lord is El Olam: the Self-Eternal God. He only relies on Himself to live. He has always been self-reliant, and He will continue to be that way throughout eternity.

God *gives to all life, breath, and all things.* God is not *worshiped with men's hands,* and He needs nothing since He is El Chuwl: the God who gave you life. You are alive today because God gives life to your body and puts breath in your lungs. You wake up each and every morning because He said so. He is the one who gives you another chance to live. Moreover, the whole universe is still in existence because He *gives to all life, breath, and all things.*

IV. Conclusion

The Lord Jesus Christ made the world and everything in it. God the Father created the whole world through Him. *For by Him all things were created that are in heaven and that are on earth, visible and invisible, whether thrones or dominions or principalities or powers. All things were created through Him and for Him* (Colossians 1:16). Given that Jesus made the whole world and everything in it, He is also Lord of heaven and earth, and He has authority over it. *All authority has been given to Me in heaven and on earth* (Matthew 28:18).

The Lord Jesus Christ also *gives to all life, breath, and all things.* Jesus died on the cross for the punishment of our sins, was buried, and rose again on the third day. Hence, He can give eternal life to anyone who repents of their sins and believes on Him for salvation. If you have yet to do so, believe on the Lord Jesus Christ today. He can forgive you of your sins and give you the gift of everlasting life.

V. Discussion Questions

1. What stood out to you about this lesson and the passages discussed?

2. When you hear, "God, who made the world and everything in it," what comes to mind? How does this truth contrast with false deities?

3. How is God *Lord of heaven and earth*? What does this tell you about His authority?

4. If the Lord isn't *worshiped with men's hands*, then how is He to be worshiped?

5. In what ways is God in need of nothing?

6. How can knowing that the Lord *gives to all life, breath, and all things* give you a greater appreciation for Him?

7. Is there anything that you can take away from this discussion and apply to your life? Any final thoughts?

Renew Their Strength

To My Sister in Christ, Hillary K.

But those who wait on the Lord shall renew their strength;
they shall mount up with wings like eagles, they shall run
and not be weary, they shall walk and not faint.

—Isaiah 40:31

I. Introduction

Has there been a time where you were worn down and then received an abundant source of energy that made you feel like a new person? Perhaps you got some rest after a long workweek. Maybe you got a second wind in the final miles of a marathon. Maybe you feel revived at dinner because you hadn't eaten all day. Perhaps you now have peace of mind after you distanced yourself from a toxic person.

These examples exhibit the process of renewal. To renew means to take up again. At some point, you feel worn down and depleted. You find it difficult to continue, and you may even be down for the count. However, you gain enough energy so you can start up again and continue your activity. You feel fresh and revived to the point that you can resume the task at hand.

II. Context

In Isaiah 40:30–31, the prophet Isaiah talked about the frailty of man. He stated that no matter who you are, you will eventually get tired and wear down: *Even the youths shall faint and be weary, and the young men shall utterly fall.* After Isaiah talked about the frailty of man, he made a transition. He listed a few of the Lord's promises in regard to renewal: *but those who wait on the Lord shall renew their strength; they shall mount up with wings like eagles, they shall run and not be weary, they shall walk and not faint.*

III. Main Points

As Isaiah proclaimed, *those who wait on the Lord shall renew their strength.* When you wait on the Lord, you're able to stay in a state of patience. You remain where you're at for His provision because you believe He will provide for your needs. You trust that He will give you the necessary components to persevere through a situation. When there is trust, there is confidence. Therefore, if you are confident in the Lord, you can patiently wait on Him.

If you wait on the Lord, you can renew your strength through the fruit of hope. When you hope for something, you anticipate that a future event may take place. When you put your hope in the Lord, you anticipate that He will come through and provide for you. *If we hope for what we do not see, we eagerly wait for it with patience* (Romans 8:25). When you're eager for something, you're excited about it. Along with the combination of anticipation and excitement, there is a new sense of life. This new sense of life can help you take up your strength again.

Also with hope comes the fruit of love. *Now hope does not disappoint, because the love of God has been poured out in our hearts by the Holy Spirit who was given to us* (Romans 5:5). If you put your hope in the Lord, He can give you strength through His love. God's love *bears all things, believes all things, hopes all things, endures all things* (1 Corinthians 13:7). With His love, you can bear the difficulties, believe that He is faithful, hope that His grace is sufficient for you, and endure until the end. Therefore, God's love can renew your strength because with it, you can remain steadfast and obedient during your season of waiting. *For this is the love of God, that we keep His commandments. And His commandments are not burdensome* (1 John 5:3).

Those who wait on the Lord *shall mount up with wings like eagles.* "Mount" is *alah* in Hebrew, which means to get up, ascend, or arise (Strong's 5927). When you mount up, you arise from a stationery state. You transition from a season of waiting into one of progression. With the guidance of the Lord, you can proceed and move forward. You're able to do so because He will lead you exactly where you need to go.

Not only will you *mount up*, but you will do so *with wings like eagles*. Eagles are known to soar high in the air and travel at fast speeds. They can soar ten thousand feet above sea level. Eagles, on average, fly at about 30 miles per hour, but can zoom up to 150 miles per hour when they dive for prey. When you *mount up with wings like eagles*, you rise up with power. You don't slowly get up and stagger around, but you arise with vigor, ready for action.[1]

Those who wait on the Lord *shall run and not be weary, they shall walk and not faint*. In order to run and not be weary, you must have stamina. To have stamina, you need to condition your body to endure. To condition your body, you must be consistent in training. To be consistent in training, you must have some form of discipline.

Likewise, the Lord can give you the ability to run and not be weary through the fruit of longsuffering. "Longsuffering" can be defined as spiritual stamina by which you demonstrate patience in the midst of hardship. The Lord develops your longsuffering through conditioning. He uses challenging situations to sanctify you, as well as to make you more like Him.

Therefore, it is important to allow the Lord to grow you on a consistent basis. You can't throw in the towel every time you don't get your way or whenever things go wrong. You should discipline yourself to study God's Word and to do what it says regardless of the situation. With discipline, you can follow the exhortation to *be still, and know that I am God* (Psalm 46:10). Stand back, rely on the power of God, and wait for His guidance. In this way, you can grow in longsuffering and not faint in adversity.

IV. Conclusion

The Lord Jesus waited on the Lord God to renew His strength. After Jesus died on the cross for the punishment of our sins, He waited three days and three nights for the Father to raise Him again from the dead. On the third day, He mounted up with wings like eagles, for He went from dead in the tomb to alive and revived. Hence, *He is risen* (Matthew 28:6).

Jesus also promised that those who believe in Him will mount up and be raised up. This is the will of Him who sent Me, that everyone who sees the Son and believes

---

1   "How Fast Eagles Fly—Wow!" Animal Food Planet, September 13, 2021, https://www.animalfoodplanet.com/how-fast-eagles-fly/.

in Him may have everlasting life; and I will raise him up at the last day (John 6:40). All believers in Christ wait for His return to the earth, when we will mount up and be resurrected in new, glorified bodies. *Behold, I tell you a mystery: We shall not all sleep, but we shall all be changed—in a moment, in the twinkling of an eye, at the last trumpet. For the trumpet will sound, and the dead will be raised incorruptible, and we shall be changed. For this corruptible must put on incorruption, and this mortal must put on immortality* (1 Corinthians 15:51–53). If you have yet to do so, believe on the Lord Jesus Christ. You will mount up with wings like an eagle, you will one day have a new, glorified body, and you will have everlasting life.

V. Discussion Questions

1. What stood out to you about this lesson and the passages discussed?

2. When you think of waiting on the Lord, what comes to mind?

3. In what ways can it be difficult to wait on the Lord?

4. What are some repercussions of not waiting on the Lord?

5. What are some ways the Lord can renew your strength?

6. *Those who wait on the Lord shall renew their strength; they shall mount up with wings like eagles, they shall run and not be weary, they shall walk and not faint.* How can the promise in Isaiah 40:31 give you hope in difficult situations?

7. Is there anything that you can take away from this discussion and apply to your life? Any final thoughts?

Faithful Are the Wounds

Dedicated to Sean R. (Market Street Mission)

Faithful are the wounds of a friend, but the
kisses of an enemy are deceitful.

—**Proverbs 27:6**

I. Introduction

Have you ever been told something that was valid, but that you didn't want to hear? For example, maybe your parents or guardians told you to eat vegetables instead of junk food so you would grow in strength and health. Perhaps a loved one advised you to stay away from a group of toxic friends who engage in delinquent behavior, the doctor told you to stay off your feet so you can recover from an injury, or your boss pointed out your weaknesses so you can improve at your job.

These are examples of the hard truth. Someone has noticed something negative in your life, whether it's bad behavior or potential danger. Because the people care about you, they present their concerns to you. Their concerns may be burdensome since it stings to hear when you are wrong or in a bad spot. It may be difficult to accept that you have a shortcoming or weakness of some sort. It's not easy to change a bad habit or give up a certain lifestyle, but if you humble yourself, listen, and make the proper adjustments, you'll be better off in the long run.

II. Context

In Proverbs 27:6, Solomon talked about the hard truth. He first described its attributes and its long-term effects. He also listed the type of people who would tell you the hard truth: *Faithful are the wounds of a friend.* The author then shifted in the opposite direction and discussed the concept of soft lies. He described what it's like, the type of people who practice it, and its effects: *but the kisses of an enemy are deceitful.*

III. Main Points

As Solomon told his audience, know that *faithful are the wounds of a friend.* The truth is faithful because it will never fail you. The truth has been tested and tried throughout the course of time. Whenever people have applied it in their lives, it has led them to the right course of action. One reason for this is that when you receive the truth, you can do an honest assessment of yourself. When you're able to look at yourself in the mirror, you can make the necessary adjustments to improve yourself, work on your flaws, and repent of any sinful behavior. Remember that *the truth shall make you free* (John 8:32). Not only does truth free you in context of salvation, but it also frees you from destructive life choices.

The truth is compared to wounds because the truth hurts. The majority of people like to be portrayed in a positive light and like to feel good about themselves. If someone provides an accurate criticism about you, it may sting. Think about it: *the word of God is living and powerful, and sharper than any two-edged sword* (Hebrews 4:12), and His *word is truth* (John 17:17). Therefore, the truth is sharper than any two-edged sword. When someone gives you the hard truth, it's as if you were verbally and emotionally sliced by a sword; hence the wounds.

The truth can come from a friend. A true friend is willing to have difficult conversations with you, and one of the reasons is that *a friend loves at all times* (Proverbs 17:17). True friends care about you and have your best interests in mind. They genuinely want to see you do well and are willing to confront you when you're wrong, even if it jeopardizes the friendship. Also, love *does not rejoice in iniquity, but rejoices in the truth* (1 Corinthians 13:6). One attribute of love is truth, which means that if your friends truly love you, they will tell you the truth.

Also take note that *the kisses of an enemy are deceitful.* Lies are like kisses because lies can be very comfortable. Just like a kiss from a spouse or partner is comforting, so a lie can be comforting since more times than not, it is what you

159

want to hear instead of what you need to hear. When you hear what you want to hear, you're more likely to feel good about yourself at that moment.

Lies come from an enemy. An enemy opposes you and doesn't want the best for you. A thief comes *to steal, and to kill, and to destroy* (John 10:10). The Enemy is like a thief because he'll use lies to steal what the Lord has planned for you. He'll use lies to kill any desires you have to walk in truth. He'll also use lies to destroy your life, as well as your relationship with the Lord. Lies are destructive since they are contrary to God's Word. Anything that contradicts God's Word is sin. Sin *brings forth death* (James 1:15). When there are lies, there is death.

Lies are deceitful because they're quite alluring. Lies can sound good to the ears and may look good on paper. Because lies can appear to be pleasant, you may be deceived and think they are good for you. You can also fall into the trap that whatever makes you feel good is actually beneficial for you. It doesn't matter if it's in violation of Scripture—as long as it feels good, then it must be right. However, *no wonder! For Satan himself transforms himself into an angel of light* (2 Corinthians 11:14). If the Father of Lies can make himself look good, you should test everything by the truth of God's Word so you don't fall into deception.

IV. Conclusion

Faithful are the wounds of the Lord Jesus Christ and His Word. It may not feel good to hear His warnings. *Unless you repent you will all likewise perish* (Luke 13:3). It can be humbling to hear that you can't do anything without Him. *Without Me you can do nothing* (John 15:5). Remember that the world hated Jesus because He called them out on their sin. The world cannot hate you, but it hates Me because I testify of it that its works are evil (John 7:7).

However, if you adhere to the absolute truth of His words, you will be well off. Therefore whoever hears these sayings of Mine, and does them, I will liken him to a wise man who built his house on the rock: and the rain descended, the floods came, and the winds blew and beat on that house; and it did not fall, for it was founded on the rock (Matthew 7:24–25). So if you have yet to do so, listen to the truth that you need Jesus to save you from your sins, as well as for everlasting life. *He who believes in the Son has everlasting life; and he who does not believe the Son shall not see life, but the wrath of God abides on him* (John 3:36).

V. Discussion Questions

1. What stood out to you about this lesson and the passages discussed?

2. When you think of the hard truth, what comes to mind?

3. Can you recall a time when you received the faithful *wounds of a friend*? What are some examples from Scripture?

4. In what ways can it be difficult to receive *the wounds of a friend*?

5. Can you recall a time when you were deceived by *the kisses of an enemy*? What are some examples from Scripture?

6. In what ways can someone be deceived by *the kisses of an enemy*?

7. Is there anything that you can take away from this discussion and apply to your life? Any final thoughts?

Lesson 38

The Kingdom of God and His Righteousness

To My Sister in Christ, Justine H.

Seek first the kingdom of God and His righteousness, and all these things shall be added to you.

—Matthew 6:33

I. Introduction

Think of something that takes precedence in your life. Perhaps it's your relationship or marriage. It's likely that you'll spend more time with your spouse than with your friends. What about work? You need money to pay the bills and buy essential items, such as food. *If anyone will not work, neither shall he eat* (2 Thessalonians 3:10). Therefore, you spend more time at work than at your hobbies. Maybe it's your schoolwork. Because your test is tomorrow, you'll allocate more time to studying instead of watching television.

These are all examples of priorities. A priority is something you consider to be more important than other things. To see something as a priority, it's likely that you see it as valuable. Because you see it as valuable, it may require more of your attention. Therefore, it's probable that you'll put something you prioritize ahead of other activities in your life.

II. Context

In Matthew 6:33, the Lord Jesus Christ gave an exhortation to His disciples. He told them where their priorities should be: *Seek first the kingdom of God and His righteousness.* Jesus then made a promise to His disciples. He promised them that their needs would be covered: *and all these things shall be added to you.*

III. Main Points

As Jesus exhorted His disciples, *seek first the kingdom of God and His righteousness.* To seek means to pursue and go after. You don't find something by random chance or accident, but you're intentional about your efforts. To seek first is to make your object of pursuit the primary target. Everything else comes afterward.

The kingdom of God is the establishment of the Lord. It's monarchical in that the Lord reigns as the one and only king. It is open to anyone who repents and believes on Him for salvation. It is territorial in that it's currently in the third heaven, but in the future will physically manifest in the millennial kingdom, as well as in the new heaven and new earth. It's eternal in that it will remain for eternity. "His righteousness" means ways that are in alignment with the standards of the Lord. It's what is morally acceptable in His sight.

To *seek first the kingdom of God and His righteousness* means to pursue the Lord wholeheartedly. Remember that the first and great commandment is to *love the Lord your God with all your heart, with all your soul, and with all your mind* (Matthew 22:37). Prioritize Him ahead of everything else. In this way, you can steer clear from idols, which can sabotage your relationship with the Lord. Doing so may also help you see the Lord as Jehovah Melek: the Lord is my King. If He is your King, submit to His ways of righteousness instead of your own ways. *Not as I will, but as You will* (Matthew 26:39).

If you *seek first the kingdom of God and His righteousness,* then *all these things shall be added to you.* When you pursue the Lord and follow Him, matters tend to take care of themselves. God promises to give you what you need—when you need it. *My God shall supply all your need according to His riches in glory by Christ Jesus* (Philippians 4:19). Because the Lord will give you what you need, He will provide you with whatever is necessary and required for you to fulfill His will.

IV. Conclusion

The Lord Jesus sought *first the kingdom of God and His righteousness.* Even from the young age of twelve, He pursued the will of His Father in heaven. When His earthly parents, Joseph and Mary, thought they had lost Him in Jerusalem, He asked them, Why did you seek Me? Did you not know that I must be about My Father's business? (Luke 2:49). Throughout His entire ministry, Jesus preached the kingdom of God and perfectly adhered to the ways of His Father, even when it cost Him His life. He *became obedient to the point of death, even the death of the cross* (Philippians 2:8).

If you have yet to do so, *seek first the kingdom of God and His righteousness* (Matthew 6:33). Repent, for the kingdom of heaven is at hand (Matthew 4:17). Turn away from your sins and seek the Lord Jesus, for He is the king of the kingdom. If you do so, *all these things shall be added to you.* If you believe on Jesus, then a relationship with God, the Holy Spirit, a glorified body, and the gift of everlasting life will be added to you.

V. Discussion Questions

1. What stood out to you about this lesson and the passages discussed?

2. When you think of seeking *first the kingdom of God,* what comes to mind?

3. What are some ways you can *seek first the kingdom of God?*

4. What are some distractions that may influence you not to *seek first the kingdom of God?*

5. What does "and all these things shall be added to you" tell you in regard to the Lord's provision?

6. Can you recall a time when you sought first the kingdom of God, and *all these things* were added to you? Can you cite an example from Scripture?

7. Is there anything that you can take away from this discussion and apply to your life? Any final thoughts?

Lesson 39

Sufficient for the Day

To My Sister in Christ, Justine H. #2

Therefore do not worry about tomorrow, for tomorrow will worry about its own things. Sufficient for the day is its own trouble.

—Matthew 6:34

I. Introduction

Have you looked so far into the future that you forgot what was currently in front of you? For example, maybe you were worried about how your team would fare in the playoffs. However, you took your focus off the remaining games on your schedule. Maybe you put all your attention on the big presentation in two weeks, but you neglected the other presentation you have in two days. Perhaps you obsess so much over the apocalypse that you no longer see the point of your daily responsibilities.

This is what you can call anticipatory anxiety. With anticipatory anxiety, you worry and fear about the future. You tend to have concerns that something negative will occur down the road. You dwell on the negative possibility so much that you convince yourself that it's inevitable. Once you've persuaded yourself that it will take place, you start to think about how you will deal with it as if it already took place. As a result, you can be consumed with something that may never occur.[1]

---

1   "5 Tips to Manage Anticipatory Anxiety," eugenetherapy.com, January 14, 2021, https://eugenetherapy.com/article/5-tips-to-manage-anticipatory-anxiety/.

II. Context

In Matthew 6:34, the Lord Jesus concluded His message on worrying. Since He promised His disciples that their needs would be met, He told them not to worry about the future: *Therefore do not worry about tomorrow*. Jesus then provided an additional reason why they shouldn't worry about tomorrow: *for tomorrow will worry about its own things*. Jesus reminded them what they should focus on: *Sufficient for the day is its own trouble*.

III. Main Points

Just as Jesus told His disciples, you, too, should *not worry about tomorrow*. Don't be overly anxious about the future. Planning ahead is a wise thing to do since you can prepare for what's ahead, but when you set all of your attention on the future, you're more likely to forget about what's in front of you. You may overlook your current situation because you are thinking about potential scenarios down the road. As a result, you lose focus on what you need to do at the moment, which can lead you astray in the wrong direction.

For instance, if you were to only stare at what's fifty feet away, you may not notice the ditch that's five feet ahead. As a result, you may fall into the ditch. If you set all your attention on the big game that is in two weeks, you may overlook the opponent you are to face next week. When you overlook an opponent, you underestimate them. When you underestimate an opponent, you're more likely to lose against them. Likewise, you can lose today's battles if you set too much of your focus on what's ahead.

Remember, *tomorrow will worry about its own things*. Your future problems may be different from the ones at the moment. *To everything there is a season, a time for every purpose under heaven* (Ecclesiastes 3:1). There will be a time and a place for you to deal with the issues that lie ahead. However, now may not be the time to deal with those issues.

If a GPS told you to make a left turn in two miles, it would make little sense to turn left at the following block that's one hundred feet away. Instead, you should wait until you cover the majority of the two-mile distance before you think about turning. Similarly, you shouldn't try to handle all your future problems today because it isn't necessary. You may want to wait until the appropriate time to take care of it.

Sufficient for the day is its own trouble. There is a good chance that there are enough issues for you to deal with today. Therefore, you should focus on the task at hand. If you focus and set your attention on your current situation, you're more likely to take care of it. Through the guidance and wisdom of the Lord, you can make sound decisions that will help you with your present circumstances, as well as glorify Him in the process.

Furthermore, the future is never guaranteed. *You do not know what will happen tomorrow. For what is your life? It is even a vapor that appears for a little time and then vanishes away* (James 4:14). You are not entitled to a long life. You can be here one day and gone the next. Take matters one day at a time since it is literally all you have.

IV. Conclusion

Jesus was not worried about tomorrow. He wasn't overly anxious about the future to the point that He lost focus on the task at hand. He knew that His heavenly Father saw His needs. Jesus knew that His Father would provide for them like He did for the plants and animals. Because He was confident about His Father's provision, He truly believed that *tomorrow will worry about its own things* (Matthew 6:34).

Jesus knew that *sufficient for the day is its own trouble.* He knew that mankind needed a Savior to save them from their sins. So every day He focused on what His Father sent Him to do, which was to destroy the works of the devil. There came a day when He died for the sins of the whole world. Because of this, we can be saved from the penalty of our sins through Him. If you have not yet done so, believe on the Lord Jesus to save you from eternal death in hell and the lake of fire. *Believe on the Lord Jesus Christ, and you will be saved* (Acts 16:31).

V. Discussion Questions

1. What stood out to you about this lesson and the passages discussed?

2. How does the Lord help you *not worry about tomorrow*?

3. What are some reasons people may *worry about tomorrow*?

4. What can be some repercussions if you overly *worry about tomorrow*?

5. *Tomorrow will worry about its own things.* How should you approach potential future problems?

6. *Sufficient for the day is its own trouble.* What are some ways to focus on the task at hand?

7. Is there anything that you can take away from this discussion and apply to your life? Any final thoughts?

Lesson 40

Glory in Tribulations

To My Sister in Christ, Sarah G.

And not only that, but we also glory in tribulations, knowing that tribulation produces perseverance.

—Romans 5:3

I. Introduction

Think of a time when you were in a difficult situation. Maybe you were bedridden with illness, or handicapped with an affliction. Perhaps you were let go from a job and couldn't seem to find any new employment. Perchance you lost something that was near and dear to you, such as a relationship, friendship, home, pet, or loved one. Maybe you've been the target of bullying at school or work.

While each of these situations presents a challenge, you can control how you respond to them. You can see your situation as all doom and gloom. You may even throw yourself a pity party. Or you can make the best of a difficult situation. You can use your difficulties as an opportunity to learn important life lessons, gain wisdom, and mature spiritually.

II. Context

In Romans 5:3–5, Paul continued to list the numerous benefits for those who have been justified by faith: *And not only that, but we also glory in tribulations*. Paul then explained why believers are able to glory in tribulations. His argument was that

170

tribulations develop godly attributes: *knowing that tribulation produces perseverance; and perseverance, character; and character, hope.* After his explanation, Paul told his audience what hope provided: *Now hope does not disappoint, because the love of God has been poured out in our hearts by the Holy Spirit who was given to us.*

III. Main Points

As Paul said to the Romans, you also can *glory in tribulations.* "Glory" is *kauchaomai* in Greek, which means to rejoice and boast (Strong's 2744). You can *rejoice always* (1 Thessalonians 5:16) and boast in the Lord, even in the midst of hardship. This doesn't mean that you always have to be happy and put on a smile when difficulties strike, but you can rejoice in the fact that the Lord will provide for your needs. You can be confident in Him since He will make a way for you to get through difficult seasons. *Many are the afflictions of the righteous, but the Lord delivers him out of them all* (Psalm 34:19).

You can glory because *tribulation produces perseverance, and perseverance, character; and character, hope.* Tribulation produces perseverance because it requires endurance to get through it. Tribulations can last for quite some time. It may continue for weeks, months, years, or possibly the rest of your life. Although tribulations can go on for some time, you can choose to rely on the strength of the Lord. With His strength, you can endure, despite adversity. Remember that the Lord is El Shaddai: the All-Powerful God. *Is there anything too hard for [Him]?* (Jeremiah 32:27).

Perseverance produces character because it helps you grow spiritually. When you persevere, you grow in longsuffering. You learn how to endure through difficult situations. You also develop patience since you learn how to wait on the Lord. If you wait on something, you trust that it will eventually come. If you wait on the Lord, your faith in Him may increase. The more you rely on Him, the more you realize that He's the only one who can get you through the storms. Therefore, *in all your ways acknowledge Him* (Proverbs 3:6).

Character produces hope because you're able to see that tribulation is temporary. If you set your focus on the Lord, you can remind yourself that the difficult season will come to an end. Also, the fruits of faith, patience, and longsuffering are based upon the premise that there is light at the end of the tunnel. Faith is based upon the belief that the Lord will get you through the difficult seasons in life. Patience is rooted in the truth that *in due season we shall reap if we do not lose heart* (Galatians 6:9). Longsuffering comes when you have a reason to press on. So *consider Him who endured such hostility from sinners against Himself, lest you grow weary and discouraged in your souls* (Hebrews 12:3).

You can glory in the fact that *hope does not disappoint, because the love of God has been poured out in our hearts by the Holy Spirit who was given to us.* "Hope" is *elpis* in Greek, which means to anticipate with pleasure (Strong's 1860). If you are in Christ, you can look forward to the day you will see Him face to face and be with Him forever. His eternal promises far exceed your temporary struggles. *Eye has not seen, nor ear heard, nor have entered into the heart of man the things which God has prepared for those who love Him* (1 Corinthians 2:9). Also, Christians are *sealed with the Holy Spirit of promise* (Ephesians 1:13). The Holy Spirit is a reminder that God loved you enough to sacrifice His Son so you can be reconciled to Him. The Holy Spirit also signifies that one day, Jesus will come again to redeem you.

IV. Conclusion

The Lord Jesus gloried in tribulations. *For the joy that was set before Him, [He] endured the cross* (Hebrews 12:2). Jesus persevered through many tribulations throughout His life. *He is despised and rejected by men, a Man of sorrows and acquainted with grief. And we hid, as it were, our faces from Him; He was despised, and we did not esteem Him. Surely He has borne our griefs and carried our sorrows; yet we esteemed Him stricken, smitten by God, and afflicted* (Isaiah 53:3–4).

Because Jesus persevered through tribulations and suffering, He developed character. He grew in the character of obedience. *Though He was a Son, yet He learned obedience by the things which He suffered* (Hebrews 5:8). Because of Jesus's obedience, there is hope for all of us. Since He was obedient unto death and rose again, salvation is available for everyone. So if you have not yet done so, repent of your sins and glorify El Hakkavod: the God of Glory. *I will praise You, O Lord my God, with all my heart, and I will glorify Your name forevermore* (Psalm 86:12).

V. Discussion Questions

1. What stood out to you about this lesson and the passages discussed?

2. How can it be difficult to *glory in tribulations*?

3. Can you recall a time when tribulation in your life produced patience? What are some examples from Scripture?

4. Can you recall a time when patience helped you grow in character? What are some examples from Scripture?

5. Can you recall a time when you grew in character, and it gave you hope? What are some examples from Scripture?

6. How has hope not disappointed you?

7. Is there anything that you can take away from this discussion and apply to your life? Any final thoughts?

To Live Is Christ

To My Brother in Christ, Brendan T. #2

For to me, to live is Christ, and to die is gain.

—Philippians 1:21

I. Introduction

Think about something that is near and dear to you. Perhaps it's your family, friends, or pets. It could be your favorite sports team. Maybe it's your job or a hobby you enjoy. It might be something you own, such as a home or a prized possession. Whatever the entity may be, you hold it in high esteem and see the value in it.

What does "value" mean? "Value" means worth. When you value something, you categorize the entity as important and of merit. The object of value has a meaningful impact on you. Therefore, you want it to be a constant in your life. The greater the impact the entity has on you, the more it can influence your decisions, beliefs, and worldview.

II. Context

In Philippians 1:21, the apostle Paul told the church at Philippi why he wanted to be bold for the Lord Jesus. He also mentioned the reason why he wanted to be a reflection of Him regardless of the circumstances. In his rationale, Paul stated how significant the Lord Jesus was to him. He proclaimed that Jesus was everything to him and that he lived his life solely for Him. *For to me, to live is Christ, and to die is gain.*

III. Main Points

As Paul said to the church of Philippi, *to live is Christ*. The Lord Jesus defines life because He is the source of it. *He gives to all life, breath, and all things* (Acts 17:25). On the physical level, He is the sole reason you're alive. You get up in the morning because He allows you to get up. You get to live another year because it's His will for you to do so.

On the spiritual level, you're made to worship Him. He made you, and therefore He is worthy of your praise. *Oh come, let us worship and bow down; let us kneel before the Lord our Maker* (Psalm 95:6). Also, the Lord Jesus is the only way to eternal life. No other gods or religions can give you that gift. *Whoever believes in Him should not perish but have everlasting life* (John 3:16).

Without Christ, life is absolutely meaningless. *Vanity of vanities, all is vanity* (Ecclesiastes 1:2). A Christless life is futile because life on earth is temporary. This means that everything on earth will eventually perish. *Heaven and earth will pass away* (Matthew 24:35; Luke 21:33). Therefore, if you live your life for anything outside of God, it will be all for not. Everything you work for will either vanish or be left behind. So remember: *you He made alive, who were dead in trespasses and sins* (Ephesians 2:1). Without Christ, you're spiritually dead; but with Him, you're spiritually revived to life.

To die is gain. To cease the continuance of something may be beneficial because there is a possibility it can be replaced with an upgrade. In the moral sense, when you die to your flesh, you depart from evil. You no longer practice sin, but you follow the Lord. Also, the less sin you consume yourself with, the more you can be filled with God's holiness. Having been set free from sin and having become slaves of God, you have your fruit to holiness, and the end is everlasting life (Romans 6:17–18).

In the eternal sense, when you die, you can get a new life. After death, you transfer to the afterlife. In the afterlife, those in Christ Jesus receive a glorified body. This is gain because the glorified body is everlasting, which means you will not experience death again. There will be no pain, suffering, or torment. Instead, there will be immortality and *pleasures forevermore* (Psalm 16:11). In the afterlife, you can be with the Lord for eternity. This is gain since you get to see Him in person. When you see someone in person, your relationship with that person may be strengthened. Many times, you *speak face to face* so that your *joy may be full* (2 John 1:12). Since you're with the Lord for eternity, your joy can be full forever and ever.

IV. Conclusion

To live is Christ. The Lord Jesus Christ came to the earth so that we can live through Him. He came to give life to those who were dead in their trespasses and sins (Ephesians 2:1). *I have come that they may have life, and that they may have it more abundantly* (John 10:10). *To die is gain.* Jesus sacrificed His life for all of us. He died on the cross to pay the punishment of all of our sins. Because of this, we can have an eternal gain that's much greater than anything the world has to offer. It has much more value than any fame, fortune, pleasure, and prestige that we could gain in this temporary life.

If you repent of your sins and believe on the Lord Jesus Christ for your salvation, you will gain an everlasting relationship with Him. Through Jesus alone, you will also gain the gift of eternal life. You will not have to go through the second death in the lake of fire. Instead, you'll get to be with the Lord forever in the new heaven and new earth. *Whoever believes in Him should not perish but have everlasting life* (John 3:16).

V. Discussion Questions

1. What stood out to you about this lesson and the passages discussed?

2. When you think of "to live is Christ," what comes to mind?

3. *To live is Christ.* How can this truth help you in the way you live?

4. In what ways is Christ correlated with life?

5. *To die is gain.* How is this truth countercultural in today's society?

6. In what ways can you gain through loss?

7. Is there anything that you can take away from this discussion and apply to your life? Any final thoughts?

At All Times

To My Brother In Christ, Lucas C. #2

A friend loves at all times, and a brother is born for adversity.

—Proverbs 17:17

I. Introduction

Have you ever had someone in your life who has been with you through thick and thin? This person not only enjoys your company in good times, but has remained with you during hardships. Perhaps they have seen your ugly side. They might have picked up on your quirks and flaws. They know your deepest and darkest secrets. Nevertheless, they made the choice to stay by your side, regardless of the circumstances.

If you had someone who has been with you through thick and thin, you may consider them to be loyal. To be loyal is to show consistent allegiance and support to an individual or group. Your commitment to someone remains steadfast. You don't let difficulties deter you from your commitment. Instead, you remain trustworthy and reliable.

II. Context

In Proverbs 17:17, Solomon described the loyalty of a friend. He first talked about how a friend can love. He also mentioned how often a friend is able to love: *A friend loves at all times.* Solomon additionally stated that a brother can be reliable.

He talked about the type of situations a brother is made for: *a brother is born for adversity.*

III. Main Points

As Solomon told his audience, *a friend loves.* A friend can be someone who associates with you and likes you for who you are. A friend can demonstrate love in various ways. For example, he or she can be patient and gentle toward you. *Love suffers long and is kind.* A friend can also be happy for you and doesn't mind if you possess something he doesn't have. *Love does not envy.* A friend can show love by not making everything about himself. *Love does not parade itself, is not puffed up* (1 Corinthians 13:4).

When a friend loves, he doesn't disrespect you. *Love does not behave rudely.* He doesn't have ulterior motives in the friendship, but genuinely cares for you. *Love does not seek its own.* A friend isn't easily set off and doesn't have ill will toward you. Love *is not provoked, thinks no evil.* A friend who loves is honest with you. He doesn't enable you, but holds you accountable and calls you out when you're wrong. Love *does not rejoice in iniquity, but rejoices in the truth* (1 Corinthians 13:5–6).

Not only does a friend love, but *a friend loves at all times*—not just when it benefits him. You show love consistently, even when it's hard or inconvenient. Remember that love *bears all things, believes all things, hopes all things, endures all things* (1 Corinthians 13:7). A friend who *loves at all times* can be steadfast in support, faith, optimism, and patience.

Also remember that *a brother is born for adversity.* A "brother" could mean a literal sibling in your family, but there are also other meanings to it. "Brother" is *ach* in Hebrew, which means affinity (Strong's 251). "Affinity" is defined as a strong connection and liking toward someone. Hence, a brother can be a fellow Christian or someone you're close to. Whether the brother is a family member or a friend, the commonality is that there's a bond between both parties.

To be born means to begin to exist, and it is correlated with creation. "A brother is born for adversity" can mean that close bonds are formed in difficult times. People can form solid relationships and help one another persevere through hardships in life. It can also mean that the people closest to you are revealed in difficult times. Do you want to see who really cares about you? Then see who stays around when you hit a low point in your life and have nothing to offer. The ones who remain close are most likely to be the brothers. Strong relationships are able to withstand trials and tribulations.

IV. Conclusion

Jesus is that friend who *loves at all times*. Throughout His ministry, Jesus demonstrated His love through patience, gentleness, and honesty. He was patient with Peter, even though he denied Him three times before the rooster crowed. He was gentle with the sinners, as well as with the tax collectors, even though they were seen as outcasts and people wanted nothing to do with them. Jesus was even honest with the Pharisees and called them out on their spiritual depravity. Most importantly, He demonstrated His love on the cross. *But God demonstrates His own love toward us, in that while we were still sinners, Christ died for us* (Romans 5:8).

If you are not yet His friend, become a friend of God. According to Jesus, *You are My friends if you do whatever I command you* (John 15:14). What does the Lord command? He *commands all men everywhere to repent* (Acts 17:30). Therefore, repent and believe on the Lord Jesus for salvation. If you do so, you will have a Friend who loves at all times, and He will be your Friend for all eternity.

V. Discussion Questions

1. What stood out to you about this lesson and the passages discussed?

2. What are some qualities you look for in a friend?

3. What are some ways that *a friend loves*?

4. How is "a friend loves at all times" different from conditional love?

5. How is "a friend loves at all times" similar to Christ's love?

6. How is a brother *born for adversity*?

7. Is there anything that you can take away from this discussion and apply to your life? Any final thoughts?

Lesson 43

Crucified with Christ

In Memory of Ms. Vera

I have been crucified with Christ; it is no longer I who live, but Christ lives in me; and the life which I now live in the flesh I live by faith in the Son of God, who loved me and gave Himself for me.

—Galatians 2:20

I. Introduction

Think of a time when someone or something has helped you out. Do you have a sense of gratitude toward your source of help? Are you grateful for your parents or guardians who raised you? Do you appreciate the teacher or coach who took the extra time to tutor you? Did you thank the pastor or church elder who mentored you? Are you thankful for the recovery program that steered you away from addiction unto sobriety? Did you give kudos to the trainer who helped you lose weight and get in shape?

If so, you might feel indebted to them. To be indebted is to be thankful and appreciative toward someone because they have helped you. You realize that a certain person or group has assisted you at some point in your life. You recognize that their help has had an impact on you. Because they have guided you in the right direction, you are grateful for them. In some cases, you may feel compelled to give back to those who have helped you, whether it's through your time, services, or finances.

II. Context

In Galatians 2:20, the apostle Paul explained to the churches of Galatia that he was indebted to the Lord Jesus Christ. He first talked about the death of his former condition: *I have been crucified with Christ.* He then mentioned that his new condition was different from his former state: *it is no longer I who live, but Christ lives in me.* Paul also stated his change in lifestyle: *and the life which I now live in the flesh I live by faith in the Son of God.* He additionally stated the reason for his change in lifestyle: *[He] loved me and gave Himself for me.*

III. Main Points

As Paul told the churches of Galatia, *I have been crucified with Christ.* When the Lord Jesus was crucified, He took on Himself the sins of mankind. *The Lord has laid on Him the iniquity of us all* (Isaiah 53:6). If you're a Christian, you don't physically crucify yourself, but you put your old lifestyle to death. You turn from a life of sin to that of holiness and sanctification. You are crucified with Christ because you experience an aspect of death with Him. He physically died on the cross so you can spiritually die to your sins.

Because *I have been crucified with Christ, it is no longer I who live, but Christ lives in me.* If you're in Christ, you depart from a carnal state. You no longer live for yourself and do what you want to do. Instead, you become born again. You have a spiritual birth, and the Holy Spirit now dwells in you. Since the Holy Spirit is the Spirit of Christ, it is Christ who lives in you.

Since *Christ lives in me, the life which I now live in the flesh I live by the faith in the Son of God.* What is faith? *Faith is the substance of things hoped for, the evidence of things not seen* (Hebrews 11:1). Although you're currently in your earthly body, you can hope and anticipate that one day you will be with the Lord Jesus in your heavenly body.

Although you physically didn't see Jesus firsthand, you can have faith in what the Scriptures said about Him because His *word is truth* (John 17:17). According to the Scriptures, Jesus *is the Son of God* (John 1:34), which means He is God made manifest in human form. Jesus has always existed, but His earthly body was conceived in Mary by the Holy Spirit.[1] So if you believe that Jesus is God, acknowl-

---

1 "What does it mean that Jesus is the Son of God?" Got Questions, accessed December 8, 2023, https://www.gotquestions.org/Jesus-Son-of-God.html.

edge Him as the supreme ruler and creator of the entire universe. If you're confident that He's your creator, honor Him in all your ways. *You are worthy, O Lord, to receive glory and honor and power; for You created all things* (Revelation 4:11).

Remember that it is *the Son of God, who loved me and gave Himself for me.* The Lord loved you well before you could love Him in return. *We love Him because He first loved us* (1 John 4:19). He demonstrated that love when He gave Himself for you. *Greater love has no one than this, than to lay down one's life for his friends* (John 15:13). Not only did the Lord Jesus lay down His life for His friends, but He did so for all of mankind, including His enemies. Because He gave His life for you, you should give your life to Him. *I beseech you therefore, brethren, by the mercies of God, that you present your bodies a living sacrifice, holy, acceptable to God, which is your reasonable service* (Romans 12:1).

IV. Conclusion

The reason we can be crucified with Christ is because He Himself was first crucified. For six hours, Jesus hung on the cross—beaten, battered, and bruised. He had thorns in His head, His hands were nailed to the cross, He was basically stripped naked, and He was mocked by the Pharisees and the Roman soldiers. For the last three hours of His crucifixion, the sun was darkened and there was darkness over all the earth.

Jesus allowed Himself to be crucified on the cross—even though He was completely innocent. Because of this, we don't have to be crucified for our sins, although we are all guilty and deserve death on a cross. Also, because Jesus was buried for three days and rose again, He is able to live in you through the Holy Spirit. If you have not yet done so, *repent therefore and be converted, that your sins may be blotted out, so that times of refreshing may come from the presence of the Lord, and that He may send Jesus Christ, who was preached to you before* (Acts 3:19–20).

V. Discussion Questions

1. What stood out to you about this lesson and the passages discussed?

2. When you think of "crucified with Christ," what comes to mind?

3. *It is no longer I who live, but Christ lives in me.* How has your life changed since you became a Christian?

4. In what ways can you *live by faith in the Son of God*? What are some challenges to this?

5. *Who loved me and gave Himself for me.* How can this truth give you a greater appreciation for the Lord?

6. In what ways can you love the Lord and give yourself to Him?

7. Is there anything that you can take away from this discussion and apply to your life? Any final thoughts?

Add to Your Faith

To My Sister in Christ, Julia S. #2

But also for this very reason, giving all diligence,
add to your faith virtue, to virtue knowledge.

—2 Peter 1:5

I. Introduction

Have you ever built upon something you already had? For example, perhaps you graduated from high school and proceeded to go for your bachelor's degree, and then for your master's degree. Maybe you received a black belt in jiujitsu, but also picked up boxing; or you're certified as a Level 1 CrossFit instructor, but your goal is to reach Level 4 certification. Maybe you learned how to play the trumpet, and now you want to learn to play the tenor saxophone.

These are instances of growth. Growth is the process of something increasing. When you have growth, you can make improvements and expand your skill set. You assess where you're currently at. In that assessment, you realize there is more to learn and achieve. You conclude that you don't want to remain stagnant and stay where you're at. Therefore, you proceed to build upon what you already have.

II. Context

In 2 Peter 1:5–7, the apostle Peter gave the churches at Asia Minor another reason why they received great promises from the Lord. He told them that the Lord's promises were given to them for encouragement. His words were meant to help them mature in the faith: *But also for this very reason, giving all diligence, add to your faith virtue, to virtue knowledge, to knowledge self-control, to self-control perseverance, to perseverance godliness, to godliness brotherly kindness, and to brotherly kindness love.*

III. Main Points

For this very reason, giving all diligence, add to your faith virtue. As with the churches at Asia Minor, you have been given the great and precious promises of the Lord all throughout Scripture. Since God has given you these promises, and He *cannot lie* (Titus 1:2), you should believe them. Because these promises are true, you should be diligent and persistent in your effort to remember them. Trusting in God's promises can help you grow in the Christian faith.

Add to your faith virtue. Virtue is good moral character. In Greek, "virtue" is *arête*, which means valor, excellence, or praise (Strong's 703). With virtue, you have the valor and courage to do what is right. Your conduct is of excellent character and will be praised by others. Virtue can stem from faith because the way you live is based upon what you believe. If you believe in God and what He says, you'll live in a way that portrays that.

Add *to virtue knowledge.* Knowledge is information. When you have information of something, you possess the details and contents of it. You can build knowledge upon virtue because if you want to do what is morally correct, you will seek ways to do so. You can read God's Word and acquire knowledge of Him, as well as of His holiness. Remember that *His way is perfect* (Psalm 18:30), which means He is the source of absolute truth and moral correctness.

Add *to knowledge self-control.* Self-control is the ability to govern yourself. With self-control, you can manage your emotions, as well as conduct yourself in a cool, calm, and collected manner. You don't explode in rage, but you channel your anger in a way that isn't sinful. With self-control, you're able to train and discipline your body to refrain from temptation. You're able to say no to the enticements of sin. Self-control can come from knowledge of the Lord since His Word approves of it. With His Word, you can know that *he who has knowledge spares his words, and a man of understanding is of a calm spirit* (Proverbs 17:27).

Add *to self-control perseverance.* Perseverance is the ability to endure despite hardship. You press on even though life may be difficult. Perseverance stems from self-control because in order to make it through a trying season, you'll need to refrain from temptation. More times than not, when you're in a difficult situation, you may want to throw in the towel or give in to sin. But with self-control, you can abstain from temptation. Refraining from temptation will help you endure through difficulties. Hence, *tribulation produces perseverance* (Romans 5:3).

Add *to perseverance godliness.* "Godliness" is *eusebeia* in Greek, which means piety and holiness (Strong's 2150). If you have godliness, you show piety, which is reverence and deep respect for the Lord. You also display holiness, which is behavior that is devoted to God and set apart from the unbelieving world. Godliness comes from perseverance because perseverance produces character (Romans 5:4). While you endure hardships, God works in you. He makes you more like Himself. As a result, you develop godly attributes and become a more accurate representation of Him.

Add *to godliness brotherly kindness.* "Brotherly kindness" is *philadelphia* in Greek, which means love for the brethren (Strong's 5360). In Scripture, brethren are fellow Christians. So when one has brotherly kindness, he or she is able to love other Christians as if they are family. Brotherly kindness can develop from godliness since it's a type of love. And because God is the definition of love, brotherly kindness is a part of God's character. As you grow in godliness and reflect God's nature, you can develop brotherly kindness.

Add *to brotherly kindness love.* This love is an agape love. It is altruistic, and one sacrifices themselves for the good of others. Agape love is genuine. It has no strings attached and asks for nothing in return. Agape love can come from brotherly kindness because they are both forms of love. What separates agape love from brotherly kindness is that agape love is the greatest form of love. *Greater love has no one than this, than to lay down one's life for his friends* (John 15:13). So if agape love is known as the greatest form of love, then it goes beyond brotherly kindness. Therefore, love for the brethren can mature into an agape love.

IV. Conclusion

Jesus grew in maturity throughout His thirty-three years on earth. When Jesus was twelve years old, He *increased in wisdom and stature, and in favor with God and men* (Luke 2:52). Up until His death, Jesus learned obedience through suffering. *Though He was a Son, yet He learned obedience by the things which He suffered* (Hebrews 5:8).

Because of Jesus's growth in maturity and His perfect obedience to God in His earthly life, He can add saving faith to your life. This is the first and most important step in regard to your maturity in the Lord. You can't add godly attributes to your faith if you don't have faith to begin with. Also, it is faith alone in Christ Jesus that saves from eternal death—and nothing else. So if you have yet to do so, *believe on the Lord Jesus Christ, and you will be saved* (Acts 16:31).

V. Discussion Questions

1. What stood out to you about this lesson and the passages discussed?

2. In what ways do you *add to your faith virtue*? What are some examples from Scripture or personal life? How can you add *to virtue knowledge*? What are some examples from Scripture or personal life?

3. In what ways can you add *to knowledge self-control*? What are some examples from Scripture or personal life?

4. How can you add *to self-control perseverance*? What are some examples from Scripture or personal life?

5. In what ways do you add *to perseverance godliness*? What are some examples from Scripture or personal life?

6. How do you add *to godliness brotherly kindness*? What are some examples from Scripture or personal life? In what ways do you add *to brotherly kindness love*? What are some examples from Scripture or personal life?

7. Is there anything that you can take away from this discussion and apply to your life? Any final thoughts?

Lesson 45

One Who Turns Away His Ear

To My Brother in Christ, Joe B.

One who turns away his ear from hearing the law, even his prayer is an abomination.

—Proverbs 28:9

I. Introduction

Have you ever disregarded something, and doing so led to problems down the road? For instance, maybe you didn't listen to the directions on the GPS, and now you're lost. Perhaps Your friends and family told you not to date that person, but you did, and you ended up in a toxic relationship that took you years to recover from. Maybe you were told not to put your hand on the stove, but you did and you got burned.

These are examples of ignoring something. To ignore means to refuse to listen to something. You are given the information first, but you choose to reject the information that was given to you. In some cases, ignoring something may not be a big deal. To ignore may even be wise if you were given bad advice; but in other cases, ignoring advice could lead to undesirable consequences.

II. Context

In Proverbs 28:9, King Solomon warned his audience about ignoring. He directed his attention toward those who didn't listen to the law: *One who turns away his ear from hearing the law*. Solomon then declared the end result for those who didn't

191

adhere to the law. He implied that those who refused to hear the law may be ignored in return: *even his prayer is an abomination.*

III. Main Points

Just as Solomon told his audience, don't be the *one who turns away his ear from hearing the law.* The one who turns away his ear is the one who refuses to listen. When you turn away your ear from something, you no longer have your attention on it. When you divert your attention away from something, it's more difficult to notice it. So if you turn away your ear from something, it's more difficult for you to hear and understand what was said. Therefore, it's easier for you to ignore it altogether.

"Law" is *torah* in Hebrew (Strong's 8451). It is often used in reference to the Decalogue, or the Ten Commandments. It's also used in relation to the Pentateuch, or the first five books of the Hebrew Bible: Genesis, Exodus, Leviticus, Numbers, and Deuteronomy. So if you turn away your ear from hearing the law, you refuse to listen to the Word of God. You ignore God's precepts and disregard His commandments.

One who turns away his ear from hearing the law, even his prayer is an abomination. Your fellowship with God will be hindered since prayer is direct communication with God. Also, "abomination" is *toebah* in Hebrew, which refers to something disgusting (Strong's 8441). Therefore, if you ignore the Lord and His commandments, there will be a disconnect between you and Him. He will find what you say to be something disgusting.

Another consequence is that your prayers will most likely be rejected. If you find something disgusting, you will either try to stay away from it or remove it altogether. Likewise, God will likely reject your prayers if He finds them detestable. They're unacceptable in His sight and He will have nothing to do with them. Know that *God does not hear sinners* (John 9:31). Also know that you should treat others the way you want to be treated. If you don't want to listen to God, then don't expect Him to listen to you.

IV. Conclusion

Jesus urged the people not to turn away their ears from hearing His messages. For instance, after Jesus told the parable of the sower, He said, *He who has ears to hear, let him hear!* (Mark 4:9). After Jesus warned the people that everything done in secret will come to light, He said, *If anyone has ears to hear, let him hear* (Mark 4:23). In Revelation, when Jesus gave His messages to the seven churches, He said, *He who has an ear, let Him hear what the Spirit says to the churches* (Revelation 2:7, 11, 29; 3:6, 13, 22).

Jesus also warned what would happen to those who turned away their ears from hearing His words: Everyone who hears these sayings of Mine, and does not do them, will be like a foolish man who built his house on the sand: and the rain descended, the floods came, and the winds blew and beat on that house; and it fell. And great was its fall (Matthew 7:26–27). Those who disobey the Lord and refuse to listen to Him will end up in hell and the lake of fire. Therefore, listen to the Lord Jesus and obey the gospel. Blessed are those who hear the word of God and keep it! (Luke 11:28).

V. Discussion Questions

1. What stood out to you about this lesson and the passages discussed?

2. Why is *hearing the law* important?

3. What are some reasons someone *turns away his ear from hearing the law?*

4. In what ways can you prevent being the *one who turns away his ear from hearing the law?*

5. *Even his prayer is an abomination.* How can this truth give you a better understanding of the Lord and His character?

6. What are some other consequences if you turn away your ear *from hearing the law?*

7. Is there anything that you can take away from this discussion and apply to your life? Any final thoughts

Be Anxious for Nothing

To My Sister in Christ, Casey A.

*Be anxious for nothing, but in everything by prayer and supplication,
with thanksgiving, let your requests be made known to God.*

—Philippians 4:6

I. Introduction

Have you ever been overwhelmed by a difficult situation? For instance, maybe you have a demanding job. The work environment is toxic and requires long hours in the office. As much as you would like to resign, you cannot do so because your job provides you with enough income to pay the bills, and you can't seem to find other employment that will pay nearly as much. Maybe you're being bullied at school. You told the perpetrator to stop, and you reported him to the school administration. However, it seems as if no one cares. Maybe you got sick and sought help from numerous doctors, but they are unable to find out what's wrong.

If the answer is yes, you might be feeling stressed. Stress is a state of tension. It's likely due to a challenging set of circumstances. You find yourself under immense pressure. The pressure never seems to go away, but only seems to increase. The amount of pressure eventually takes a toll on you. You begin to become fatigued physically, mentally, and emotionally—and you may even start to worry about how you will make it through your situation.

II. Context

In Philippians 4:6, the apostle Paul gave instructions to the church at Philippi about what they should do in any situation. He started his statement with what they shouldn't do: *Be anxious for nothing.* Paul continued his statement with what they should do. He told them how they should proceed in their circumstances: *but in everything by prayer and supplication, with thanksgiving.* Paul finished his statement with an exhortation: *let your requests be made known to God.*

III. Main Points

As Paul told the church at Philippi, *be anxious for nothing.* When you're anxious, you worry about something that may be undesirable. There's a possibility that you'll take your focus off the Lord and forget that He will preserve you through your difficulties. Instead, you may set your attention on how problematic your situation is. If you focus on how big your problems are, you could let them have power over you. When you let something have power over you, it can control your thoughts and actions and may leave you with a defeated mindset. You may even give up on your situation altogether.

Because anxiety can paralyze you into defeat, it is imperative that you don't give in to it. *God has not given us a spirit of fear, but of power and of love and of a sound mind* (2 Timothy 1:7). Anything that isn't from God is of Satan and his forces of evil. So when you sense fear and anxiety about a certain situation, know that it isn't from the Lord. It could be Satan's attempt to stop you in your tracks.

Be anxious for nothing, but in everything by prayer and supplication. If you feel overly stressed about a situation, take it to God in prayer. Prayer is how you communicate to God. Although He knows your thoughts and understands what is in your heart, He wants to hear it from you. When you open up to the Lord and tell Him your troubles, you show humility. You admit that you can't do everything on your own and that you need Him to persevere. Also, humility is a part of Jesus's character. He is *lowly in heart* (Matthew 11:29). If you can humble yourself before the Lord in prayer, you reflect more of His character.

Your prayers and supplications should be *with thanksgiving.* "Thanksgiving" is *eucharista* in Greek, which means gratitude or grateful language (Strong's 2169). You should pray to the Lord in a spirit of gratitude because He is the creator of all things. Because He *created all things* (Revelation 4:11), He deserves your honor and respect. Remember that *He who built the house has more honor than the house*

(Hebrews 3:3). Think about it—the creator of the universe has granted you the opportunity to speak to Him. Therefore, you should speak to Him in a grateful manner.

Let your requests be made known to God. While it is important to pray, the object of your prayer is equally important. If you pray all day to a false deity, what good does that do? *They have ears, but they do not hear; nor is there any breath in their mouths* (Psalm 135:17). Because these gods are lifeless, they can't hear your prayers. Since they can't hear your prayers, your requests will go unanswered. It is a waste of time to pray to something that cannot hear or answer you. Therefore, pray to the Lord because He is El Chai: the Living God. He is alive and can hear the prayers of the righteous. So cast *all your care upon Him, for He cares for you* (1 Peter 5:7).

IV. Conclusion

There were instances when Jesus was anxious, but He didn't let that anxiety paralyze Him. *By prayer and supplication,* He made His requests known to the Father. At the garden of Gethsemane, before Jesus got arrested, He was in so much agony that He prayed until He bled. *And being in agony, He prayed more earnestly. Then His sweat became like great drops of blood falling down to the ground* (Luke 22:44).

Although Jesus might have been anxious about the suffering He was about to endure, He still prayed, O My Father, if it is possible, let this cup pass from Me; nevertheless, not as I will, but as You will (Matthew 26:39). It was the Father's will for Him to die on the cross to bear the punishment for our sins. Because of this, we can be made known to God if we repent and believe in the gospel of Jesus Christ. If you have yet to do so, call upon the Lord in prayer, for whoever calls on the name of the Lord shall be saved (Joel 2:32; Acts 2:21; Romans 10:13).

V. Discussion Questions

1. What stood out to you about this lesson and the passages discussed?

2. When you think of "be anxious for nothing," what comes to mind?

3. How can it be difficult to *be anxious for nothing*?

4. *But in everything by prayer and supplication.* How is prayer important?

5. *But in everything by prayer and supplication, with thanksgiving.* Why is the way you pray important?

6. *Let your requests be made known to God.* Why is who you pray to important?

7. Is there anything that you can take away from this discussion and apply to your life? Any final thoughts?

The Peace of God

To My Sister in Christ, Casey A. #2

And the peace of God, which surpasses all understanding,
will guard your hearts and minds through Christ Jesus.

—Philippians 4:7

I. Introduction

Have you ever been in a challenging situation, but were able to remain at ease? Perhaps you suffered a severe injury, but kept calm throughout the entire recovery phase. Maybe you lost your job and the bills piled up. Although finances were tight, you didn't panic. Perchance you were ditched by a group of friends. Even though you could have remained angry, you forgave them and moved on with your life.

If you are able to remain at ease in a challenging situation, then you have composure. Composure is the ability to stay calm in the midst of hardship. You find yourself in a difficult circumstance, and things don't look too good; however, a sense of peace overcomes you. You may not know how things will turn out, but you're able to remain steadfast regardless of the results.

II. Context

In Philippians 4:7, Paul shared a promise from the Lord based upon the exhortation in the previous verse. He told the church at Philippi that if they were consistent in prayer and went to the Lord with thanksgiving, they would receive the peace of God. Paul also mentioned the effects that God's peace would have on them: *and the peace of God, which surpasses all understanding, will guard your hearts and minds through Christ Jesus.*

III. Main Points

As Paul told the church at Philippi, *the peace of God . . . surpasses all understanding.* "Peace" is *eirere* in Greek, which means quietness and rest (Strong's 1515). With peace, there can be quietness in the midst of turbulence and rest in the face of turmoil. One reason for this is that peace tends to have a calming effect—and since it stems from the Lord, it's called *the peace of God.*

The peace of God . . . surpasses all understanding since it exceeds the comprehension of the human mind. The Lord is the *Prince of Peace* (Isaiah 9:6), which means He is the head person and ruler over peace. Since the Lord is the ruler of peace, His peace will always be more abundant than any other form of peace. It is ever-present, which means it is always there, even in the direst of circumstances. Because it is ever-present, it surpasses and goes beyond the temporary peace of man. Hence, *may the Lord of peace Himself give you peace always in every way* (2 Thessalonians 3:16).

Since *the peace of God surpasses all understanding,* [it] *will guard your hearts and minds.* To guard means to protect from danger or a threat. When you're in a difficult situation, your heart and mind are susceptible to attacks. Your mind could be plagued with evil thoughts and your heart can draw you into temptation. But God's peace can protect you since it helps you keep your composure, even when something tries to pull you astray.

The peace of God . . . will guard your hearts and minds through Christ Jesus. "Through" can be defined as the agent by which something is completed. The Lord Jesus is the agent by whom you can receive the peace of God. If you believe in Him, you have the Holy Spirit, which Jesus considers to be His peace. *Peace I leave with you, My peace I give to you* (John 14:27). Peace was also created through Him. Remember—*all things were created through Him and for Him* (Colossians 1:16). All things were created through the Lord Jesus, and this includes peace.

IV. Conclusion

Jesus is known as the *Prince of Peace* (Isaiah 9:6). He came to earth to restore the broken relationship between mankind and God. He *made peace through the blood of His cross* (Colossians 1:20). Through His death, burial, and resurrection, there no longer has to be enmity between us and God. *For if when we were enemies we were reconciled to God through the death of His Son, much more, having been reconciled, we shall be saved by His life* (Romans 5:10).

If you do not yet know God's peace, you can have *the peace of God, which surpasses all understanding*, through faith in the Lord Jesus Christ. *Therefore, having been justified by faith, we have peace with God through our Lord Jesus Christ* (Romans 5:1). If you believe in Him, *He Himself [will be your] peace* (Ephesians 2:14). He will give you the peace of the Holy Spirit, which will keep your hearts and minds through Him.

V. Discussion Questions

1. What stood out to you about this lesson and the passages discussed?

2. When you think of *the peace of God*, what comes to mind?

3. In what ways is *the peace of God* different from all other forms of peace?

4. Can you recall a time when *the peace of God* guarded your heart and mind? If so, how?

5. How can *the peace of God* give you a greater appreciation of the Lord?

6. How does *the peace of God* point to Jesus?

7. Is there anything that you can take away from this discussion and apply to your life? Any final thoughts?

Lesson 48

By My Spirit

To My Brother in Christ, Steve E.

So he answered and said to me: "This is the word of the Lord to Zerubbabel: 'Not by might nor by power, but by My Spirit,' says the Lord of hosts."

—Zechariah 4:6

I. Introduction

Reflect on a time when you completed a task, but it wasn't done on your own. For example, maybe your friends helped you move into your new place or your coworkers helped you finish a work project by the deadline. Perhaps the company's profits increased exponentially through the excellent work of the employees. Maybe you won the 4 x 400 meter relay race in track, which you couldn't have done without your teammates.

If you have competed something through the help of others, then you have received assistance. Assistance is the act of helping and supporting another party. If you receive assistance from others, the ability to do something is likely to increase. This is due to the addition of intellect, manpower, and strength. Remember that *two are better than one, because they have a good reward for their labor* (Ecclesiastes 4:9). You're able to accomplish a lot more with help, and there are even situations when you can't complete an action unless you have assistance from an outside source.

II. Context

In Zechariah 4:6, an angel interpreted the fifth of eight visions to the prophet Zechariah. The angel told him that the vision was about Zerubbabel, the governor of Judea and the leader of the first exodus from Babylonian captivity. He told Zechariah that Zerubbabel would fulfill a future prophecy in regard to the second temple. He also said that Zerubbabel would not fulfill the prophecy in his own strength, but through the Lord's assistance. *"This is the word of the Lord to Zerubbabel: 'Not by might nor by power, but by My Spirit,' says the Lord of hosts."*

III. Main Points

Like the Lord's prophecy of Zerubbabel, it is *not by might nor by power*. "By" is the way an action is completed. It's the method in which something is done. Might and power are synonymous with physical strength. It is the ability to do an action. Therefore, if it's *not by might nor by power*, it means you're unable to complete things on your own accord. It is not through your sole capabilities that it gets done.

It is *not by might nor by power* due to physical limitations. *Without Me you can do nothing* (John 15:5). When the Lord isn't in the picture, you're unable to complete a single task. This includes the bare necessities of life, such as eating, sleeping, and breathing. Since you're not able to do what is needed to live on your own, you would be a lifeless corpse without the Lord's intervention.

It's *not by might nor by power* because of spiritual limitations. If you think you can do things on your own, there is a tendency to get prideful. You may rely on yourself instead of on the Lord. You may start to believe the lie that you don't need God in order to do a certain task. This lie can progress to a complete dismissal of God in your life. Therefore, humble yourself with the truth that *he who trusts in his own heart is a fool* (Proverbs 28:26). By doing so, you will not be led astray by wicked thoughts or desires.

It's *not by might nor by power, but by My Spirit*. The "but" signals a change in direction. It hints at a contrast to what has been stated. "Might" and "power" are contrasted with "My Spirit," as indicated by "but." Therefore, it is a revelation as to the way something is done. *My Spirit* is in reference to the Spirit of the Lord. Therefore, when you seek to partake in an action, you should do it through the Lord. When you do, God can guide you with the Holy Spirit in the way you should go. He is the Helper who *will teach you all things, and bring to your remembrance all things that [He] said to you* (John 14:26).

It is *by My Spirit* because through the Lord you can accomplish the task at hand. "Spirit" is *ruwach* in Hebrew, which means "breath" (Strong's 7307). Breath is a symbol of life. Hence, when something is done by the Lord's Spirit, He gives life to the action. This means that if you do something by the Holy Spirit, the Lord gives you the ability to complete the action. Remember that the Lord *gives to all life, breath, and all things* (Acts 17:25). It's only through Him that you can do it.

IV. Conclusion

Jesus couldn't do anything by His own might or power. He got all of His ability from the God the Father. *Most assuredly, I say to you, the Son can do nothing of Himself, but what He sees the Father do; for whatever He does, the Son does in like manner* (John 5:19). Even the words Jesus spoke were from the Father. *The words that I speak to you I do not speak on My own authority; but the Father who dwells in Me does the works* (John 14:10).

By the Spirit of the Lord, Jesus was able to do His ministry on the earth. *The Spirit of the Lord is upon me, Because He has anointed Me to preach the gospel to the poor; He has sent Me to heal the brokenhearted, To proclaim liberty to the captives And recovery of sight to the blind, To set at liberty those who are oppressed; To proclaim the acceptable year of the Lord* (Luke 4:18-19). If you repent and believe in the gospel, you will receive the Lord's Spirit. *Repent, and let every one of you be baptized in the name of Jesus Christ for the remission of sins; and you shall receive the gift of the Holy Spirit* (Acts 2:38).

V. Discussion Questions

1. What stood out to you about this lesson and the passages discussed?

2. What are some ways you try to do things *by might [or] by power*? What are some examples from Scripture?

3. How can it be tempting to do things *by might [or] by power*?

4. What are some consequences if you try to do things *by might [or] by power*? What are some examples from Scripture?

5. How can you do something *by My Spirit*?

6. How can doing something *by My Spirit* help you grow in your relationship with the Lord?

7. Is there anything that you can take away from this discussion and apply to your life? Any final thoughts?

Lesson 49

Appeared to All Men

To My Brother in Christ, Joel W.

*For the grace of God that brings salvation
has appeared to all men.*

—Titus 2:11

I. Introduction

Think of something that's accessible and obtainable by most, if not all, people. For instance, oxygen is present to everyone and can be taken in by breathing. Eighty-one percent of the world's population has access to safe drinking water.[1] Most people wear some form of clothing. It can either be purchased from a supplier or crafted at home. Music is available throughout the world. It can be produced by our voice, and it can be listened to with our ears.

These are instances of things that are available. "Available" is defined as an object or entity that's present. It's there at the same time as you, and you're able to recognize it. It's also noted as something that can be accessed, obtained, or received. Either you can get hold of the entity or someone may give it to you.

---

1   "Billions of people will lack access to safe water, sanitation and hygiene in 2030 unless progress quadruples—warn WHO, UNICEF," Unicef.com, July 1, 2021, https://www.unicef.org/press-releases/ billions-people-will-lack-access-safe-water-sanitation-and-hygiene-2030-unless.

II. Context

In Titus 2:11, the apostle Paul explained to Timothy why he urged the church at Crete to live in righteousness. Paul started his explanation with a component that leads to holy living: *the grace of God*. He also mentioned what the grace of God does: *brings salvation*. Paul then stated who the grace of God is available to: it *has appeared to all men*.

III. Main Points

Follow the same exhortation that Paul mentioned to Titus to live righteously *for the grace of God*. "Grace" is known as unmerited favor. When something is unmerited, you didn't earn it. Favor can be supported through acts of kindness. Therefore, the grace of God is when you receive kindness and support from the Lord even though you did nothing to deserve it.

For the grace of God that brings salvation. "To bring" is to have something in your possession as you move to another location. "Salvation" is deliverance and perseverance from harm. Hence, the grace of God brings deliverance from eternal death, as well as perseverance through eternal life. *For by grace you have been saved through faith, and that not of yourselves: it is the gift of God, not of works, lest anyone should boast* (Ephesians 2:8–9).

Salvation has appeared to all men. Salvation has appeared in the sense that the Lord has made it available. People can read about it in the Holy Scriptures, as well as hear of it from friends, family members, pastors, evangelists, and strangers. The Lord has offered salvation so that those who believe in Him can receive it.

All men refers to everybody from every nation on earth. The Lord's gift of grace has been presented to both Israel—God's physical people, and the gentiles—the non-Jewish population. *Salvation has appeared to all men* because the Lord is *not willing that any should perish but that all should come to repentance* (2 Peter 3:9). He wants to save everybody from hell. Since the Lord wants to save everybody, He desires you to be saved!

IV. Conclusion

The grace of God that brings salvation appeared through Jesus Christ. *For the law was given through Moses, but grace and truth came through Jesus Christ* (John 1:17). The grace of God that brings salvation appeared when Jesus came to earth.

The Word became flesh and dwelt among us, and we beheld His glory, the glory as of the only begotten of the Father, full of grace and truth (John 1:14).

It was by the grace of God that Jesus died for all men. *But we see Jesus, who was made a little lower than the angels, for the suffering of death crowned with glory and honor, that He, by the grace of God, might taste death for everyone* (Hebrews 2:9). Because of Jesus's death on the cross, God's grace that brings salvation *has appeared to all men.* If you have not yet done so, receive the grace of God today. *We then, as workers together with Him also plead with you not to receive the grace of God in vain. For He says: "In an acceptable time I have heard you, and in the day of salvation I have helped you." Behold, now is the accepted time; behold, now is the day of salvation* (2 Corinthians 6:1–2).

V. Discussion Questions

1. What stood out to you about this lesson and the passages discussed?

2. When you think of the grace of God, what comes to mind?

3. How can the grace of God give you a greater appreciation and understanding of Him?

4. In what ways does the grace of God bring salvation? How is this different from a works-based salvation?

5. *For the grace of God that brings salvation has appeared to all men.* How is the gospel inclusive to everyone?

6. How is the inclusivity of the gospel different from universalism? (Universalism is the belief that everyone will eventually be saved. All roads lead home.)

7. Is there anything that you can take away from this discussion and apply to your life? Any final thoughts?

Lesson 50

Commit Your Works

To My Brother in Christ, Chris L.

Commit your works to the Lord, and your thoughts will be established.

—Proverbs 16:3

I. Introduction

Think about all the activities you do. Who are they for? For example, you exercise to improve your health. You work a full-time job so you can make enough money to provide for your family. You composed a song in honor of a loved one. You put in extra time at basketball practice so you can help your team win games. You donated food and clothing to assist those in need.

The examples above are acts of dedication. If you dedicate something, you do it for a specific purpose. You recognize that something is of importance or necessity to you. Because you believe it is important, you allocate your time, energy, and efforts toward it. You plan how you want to go about it, and then you execute the plan.

II. Context

In Proverbs 16:3, King Solomon issued an "if-then" statement in regard to dedication. He started the statement with a condition: *Commit your works to the Lord.* He finished the statement with a promise. He believed that if a person committed their works to the Lord, then a certain outcome would likely happen. He was convinced that the outcome would affect the way they think: *and your thoughts will be established.*

III. Main Points

As Solomon told his audience, *commit*. One definition of "commit" is to give of yourself to something. It is a combination of intentionality, action, and consistency. It is intentional since you need to set your focus on a target. Otherwise, how do you know what you want to commit to? It requires action because things aren't going to happen on their own. It involves consistency because you need to be consistent in your actions in order to continue or complete what you want to do.

Since commitment involves focus and persistence, it could lead to an increase in diligence. Diligence usually leads to desired results. *The soul of the diligent shall be made rich* (Proverbs 13:4). If you are diligent, there's a possibility you might be materially rich in finances. However, it is more likely that you'll be spiritually rich in godly character and attributes.

Commit your works. Have a purpose in your actions. Know what you want to do and why you want to do it. In this way, you can have stability with clarity and direction. When there's clarity and direction in what you want to do, you're more likely to stay motivated. You can remind yourself of the rationale behind your actions. Hence, you can keep your eyes on the prize.

Commit your works to the Lord. Dedicate your life to the Lord God Almighty. He should be the main factor behind what you do, for He created you, as well as all things. Since He created you, He is worthy of your dedication. Also, you were created to serve Him. *You are worthy, O Lord, to receive glory and honor and power; for you created all things, and by Your will they exist and were created* (Revelation 4:11).

Commit your works to the Lord, and your thoughts will be established. If you dedicate your life to the Lord and desire to honor Him with your deeds, He will make a way for you to do so. One way He can help you honor Him is through your thoughts. Thoughts are when you form ideas, opinions, and beliefs through your thinking.

The Lord can form your thoughts through His Word. *Knowledge of the Holy One is understanding* (Proverbs 9:10). Through the Word, you can acquire more knowledge about the Lord and what is pleasing to Him. If you fill your mind with His Word, then your ideas, opinions, and beliefs will more likely be rooted in Him. Therefore, *brethren, whatever things are true, whatever things are noble, whatever things are just, whatever things are pure, whatever things are lovely, whatever things are of good report, if there is any virtue and if there is anything praiseworthy—meditate on these things* (Philippians 4:8).

IV. Conclusion

The Lord Jesus was quite committed. He was committed to the will of God the Father: *For I have come down from heaven, not to do My own will, but the will of Him who sent Me* (John 6:38). He was committed to save people from their sins: *Those who are well have no need of a physician, but those who are sick. I did not come to call the righteous, but sinners, to repentance* (Mark 2:17).

Because Jesus was committed to the will of His Father, He committed His works to Him as well. He lived a perfect life, fully devoted to God. When He was crucified on the cross for our sins, He committed His spirit to the Lord: *And when Jesus had cried out with a loud voice, He said, "Father, 'into Your hands I commit My spirit'"* (Luke 23:46). Because Jesus committed His works to the Lord and died for the punishment of our sins, we ought to commit our works to Him. So if you have yet to do so, commit your works to the Lord. Repent from your sins and live a life dedicated to the Lord Jesus Christ. *Let your heart therefore be loyal to the Lord our God, to walk in His statutes and keep His commandments, as at this day* (1 Kings 8:61).

V. Discussion Questions

1. What stood out to you about this lesson and the passages discussed?

2. When you think of the word "commit," what comes to mind?

3. How can the Christian walk be a commitment?

4. What are some reasons to *commit your works to the Lord?*

5. In what ways can you *commit your works to the Lord?*

6. How can your thoughts be influenced by what you commit to?

7. Is there anything that you can take away from this discussion and apply to your life? Any final thoughts?

In Hope, in Tribulation, in Prayer

To My Sister in Christ, Mary C.

Rejoicing in hope, patient in tribulation, continuing steadfastly in prayer.

—Romans 12:12

I. Introduction

Think about somewhere or something in which you are a participant. This could be an event, such as a meeting, game, or concert. It can be a group, such as a workplace, band, club, or circle of friends. Perhaps it's a geographic location, such as a town, county, or state. Maybe it's financial status, such as credit or debt. Perchance it is a state of affairs, such as peace, prosperity, pain, or perdition.

These are some examples of things that you could be involved in. The term "in" is the expression of an entity that's surrounded by something else. You may be there, but another thing is present with you, and it encircles you with its presence. Because it surrounds you, it plays a current part in your life. Since it plays a part in your life, ask yourself: What part do I play in it?

II. Context

In Romans 12:12, the apostle Paul listed a third set of instructions in regard to how the Christians at Rome can have brotherly love for one another. In this particular set, Paul told them what they should do in certain situations. He told them what to do when they feel hopeful: *rejoicing in hope*. He told them how to respond to adversity: *patient in tribulation*. He told them what to do in all situations: *continuing steadfastly in prayer*.

III. Main Points

As Paul told the church at Rome, be *rejoicing in hope*. "Rejoice" means to show great pleasure and happiness. Hope is the anticipation of something desirable in the future. Therefore, *rejoicing in hope* is when you show great delight in something you look forward to. You can have faith that a desirable event may happen in the future, and because you have faith in that possibility, you can be excited about it.

You should be *rejoicing in hope* because of the Lord's promises. The Lord promises eternal life: *Whoever believes in [Me] should not perish but have everlasting life* (John 3:16). The Lord promises no more suffering: *God will wipe away every tear from their eyes; there shall be no more death, nor sorrow, nor crying. There shall be no more pain, for the former things have passed away* (Revelation 21:4). Since God *cannot lie* (Titus 1:2), you can look forward to God fulfilling His promises, and you can be excited about it.

Be *patient in tribulation*. Patience is the ability to remain calm, cool, and collected for an extended period of time. Tribulation is a period of distress and difficulty. Therefore, to be *patient in tribulation* is to remain calm in moments of trouble. Although a season of distress may take place, you don't go into a panic. Instead, you wait and rely on the strength of the Lord to get you through.

You should be *patient in tribulation* because of the quality of the afterlife. Better days lie ahead for those who put their faith in the Lord. *The sufferings of this present time are not worthy to be compared with the glory which shall be revealed in us* (Romans 8:18). Keep in mind that the troubles you go through are temporary. They may not be easy, pleasant, or fun, but they will eventually come to an end. Also, patience leads to spiritual growth. Therefore, *let patience have its perfect work, that you may be perfect and complete, lacking nothing* (James 1:4).

Be *continuing steadfastly in prayer*. When you continue steadfastly in an activity or behavior, you make it a constant in your life. Regardless of the circumstances, you continue with the task at hand. Prayer is the way you communicate to God. Therefore, if you continue steadfastly, you're persistent in your communication with God, speaking to Him on a consistent basis.

You should continue *steadfastly in prayer* because communication is necessary in every relationship. In order for a relationship to flourish, you must know how to speak to your partner and listen to him. If you don't speak to the person, how is he or she supposed to know what is on your mind and connect with you? Although God knows your thoughts, He wants you to express them to Him. In this way, you can grow in the godly character of humility and can learn to rely on Him more.

You should be *continuing steadfastly in prayer* because it's a way to serve Him. There are numerous instances throughout Scripture when we are told to pray to God. For example, we are to *pray without ceasing* (1 Thessalonians 5:17), and we are to always *pray and not lose heart* (Luke 18:1). If you follow the Lord's command to pray, then you are being obedient to His exhortation. Obedience is a form of worship to the Lord. Therefore, *if you love [God], keep [His] commandments* (John 14:15). Keep His commandment to *pray without ceasing.*

IV. Conclusion

The Lord Jesus rejoiced in hope. He rejoiced that the hope of salvation was made known to His disciples. *In that hour Jesus rejoiced in the Spirit and said,* "I thank You, Father, Lord of heaven and earth, that You have hidden these things from the wise and prudent and revealed them to babes. Even so, Father, for so it seemed good in Your sight (Luke 10:21). Jesus was patient in tribulation. Although He could have called twelve legions of angels to strike the Pharisees and Roman soldiers dead (Matthew 26:53), He held His peace. *He was oppressed and He was afflicted, yet He opened not His mouth; He was led as a lamb to the slaughter, and as a sheep before its shearers is silent, so He opened not His mouth* (Isaiah 53:7).

Jesus continued steadfastly in prayer. Through His entire ministry on earth, He made it a priority to pray to His Father in heaven. Jesus prayed all night before He chose His disciples: *Now it came to pass in those days that He went out to the mountain to pray, and continued all night in prayer to God* (Luke 6:12). Jesus prayed for the perseverance of His disciples: I do not pray that You should take them out of the world, but that You should keep them from the evil one (John 17:15). Jesus also prayed that His Father's will would be done, and Jesus fulfilled His Father's will when He died on the cross for the punishment of our sins. Because of this, anyone who believes on Him can rejoice in the hope of salvation through Him and receive the promise of everlasting life. Whoever believes in Him should not perish but have everlasting life (John 3:16).

V. Discussion Questions

1. What stood out to you about this lesson and the passages discussed?

2. How can hope help you rejoice?

3. What are some situations in which you can rejoice in hope?

4. What are some challenges to being *patient in tribulation*?

5. What are some examples from Scripture when someone was *patient in tribulation*?

6. In what ways is *continuing steadfastly in prayer* important?

7. Is there anything that you can take away from this discussion and apply to your life? Any final thoughts?

Lesson 52

My Strength

To My Sister in Christ, Ms. Dorice #2

I will love You, O Lord, my strength.

—Psalm 18:1

I. Introduction

Think of something that can move a heavy weight or withstand a lot of resistance. Take powerlifters for example. A 200-pound elite powerlifter can bench more than 380 pounds, squat about 500 pounds, and deadlift more than 565 pounds.[1] Elephants can carry up to about 19,800 pounds, which is the average weight of 130 grown adults. Gorillas can lift ten times their bodyweight and are fifteen times stronger than humans.[2]

All of these examples are demonstrations of strength. Strength is the quality of being strong. "Strong" is defined as the ability to move heavy weight. It's also the ability to withstand a lot of pressure and resistance. Although there are numerous examples in which something demonstrates strength, ask yourself this: Where does your strength come from? Does it come from lifting weights, mental fortitude, or something beyond that?

---

1   https://strengthlevel.com/.
2   "The Strongest Animals in the World," Safaris Africana, https://safarisafricana.com/strongest-animals-in-the-world/.

II. Context

In Psalm 18:1–3, David praised the Lord because He had delivered him from Saul and all his enemies. He started his song with a promise and an acknowledgement that the Lord is his strength: *I will love You, O Lord, my strength.* David then talked about how the Lord is strong enough to protect Him: *The Lord is my rock and my fortress and my deliverer; my God, My strength, in whom I will trust; my shield and the horn of my salvation, my stronghold.* David also mentioned what he planned to do, as well as his confidence in the Lord: *I will call upon the Lord, who is worthy to be praised; so shall I be saved from my enemies.*

III. Main Points

Like David, proclaim, *I will love You, O Lord, my strength.* "Will" is a declaration of a future action that is to take place. Every Christian should love the Lord now and in the future. Why? Because He created you to serve Him. Also, it's the first and great commandment of His law. *Love the Lord your God with all your heart, with all your soul, and with all your mind* (Matthew 22:37). You should love the Lord through obedience because it's His love language. It's how He receives love from you. *If you love Me, keep My commandments* (John 14:15). You should also acknowledge the Lord as Elohay Mauzi: the Lord is My Strength. He is our strength because He is omnipotent, which means He has the power to do anything He pleases.

The Lord is my rock and my fortress and my deliverer. The rock, fortress, and deliverer show commonality because they can provide protection. "Rock" is *cela* in Hebrew, which means craggy rock (Strong's 5553). Craggy rocks provide protection since they have a steep slope, as well as a rough and jagged texture. A large number of craggy rocks are clustered together at the same location, so it would be rather difficult to get through them without a scratch. Fortresses provide protection since their walls are high and sturdy. This makes it tough to climb over or to barge through. A deliverer's main goal is to save someone or a group of people from further harm. Hence, they can provide protection from danger.

These physical examples of protection symbolize the Lord since He can provide spiritual protection. He can use His angels to protect you from your enemies. *He shall give His angels charge over you, to keep you in all your ways. In their hands they shall bear you up, lest you dash your foot against a stone* (Psalm 91:11–12). The only reason you face attacks is because God allows the Enemy to attack you.

Think about Job for example. Satan had to get God's permission to attack him. Also, one name for God is Jehovah Magen: the Lord is My Shield and Protector. Protection is a part of God's character.

My God, my strength, in whom I will trust. "Trust" is *chasah* in Hebrew, which means to flee for protection (Strong's 2620). "Trust" also means confidence in the reliability of something. If you think something is reliable, then you're more likely to trust in it. For example, if you have driven the same car for two years and it has yet to break down, you're more likely to trust that it will get you to your destination safely. Likewise, you can flee to the Lord for protection and trust in Him because His strength will never fail. He may not protect you from every attack, but He can give you the strength to get through each one.

My shield and the horn of my salvation, my stronghold. A shield, a horn, and a stronghold are all items used in battle. Each of them has a specific purpose. A shield is a portable item of armor used to defend yourself against an opponent's attack. In ancient Israel, the shofar, or ram's horn, was used to rally the troops and prepare them for battle. A stronghold is a military facility built to withstand attacks from the enemy.

As the shield, horn, and stronghold were used in physical battle, so the Lord can help you in spiritual battle. He shields you with His truth. *His truth shall be your shield and buckler* (Psalm 91:4). Also, "horn" is *qeren* in Hebrew, which means power or ray of light (Strong's 7161). A ray of light can signify hope. So not only can the Lord prepare you for spiritual battle, but He may also give you a ray of hope in the midst of it. He can give you the power to get through the battle. Additionally, the Lord can be a stronghold in times of adversity. *The Lord also will be a refuge for the oppressed, a refuge in times of trouble* (Psalm 9:9).

I will call upon the Lord, who is worthy to be praised; so shall I be saved from my enemies. To call upon the Lord is to pray or sing praise to Him. He is worthy to be praised for a countless number of reasons. One of them is for His ability to save from harm. With the Lord, you can be saved from your enemies. Also, in this context, "so" is a conjunction, which explains the reason why David will call to the Lord—so the Lord will hear, respond, and save him from his enemies. Therefore, call upon the Lord so that He may hear, respond, and save you from your enemies. While it's true that the Lord knows your every thought, He wants you to humble yourself and confess your thoughts to Him. Remember that *God resists the proud, but gives grace to the humble* (James 4:6).

IV. Conclusion

We can love Jesus because He first loved us. *We love Him because He first loved us* (1 John 4:19). He demonstrated His love for us when He laid down His life for us. Jesus can be our strength. His strength is *made perfect in weakness* (2 Corinthians 12:9). Jesus can be our rock and fortress. He is known as that spiritual Rock that followed the Israelites in the days of Moses (1 Corinthians 10:4). He is also known as the chief cornerstone: *Behold, I lay in Zion a chief cornerstone, elect, precious, and he who believes on Him will by no means be put to shame (1 Peter 2:6). Jesus is our deliverer because He saves us from our sins, as well as from hell. When John the Baptist saw Jesus, he said, Behold! The Lamb of God who takes away the sin of the world!* (John 1:29). We can trust in Jesus because He is always faithful and will never change. *Jesus Christ is the same yesterday, today, and forever* (Hebrews 13:8).

If we believe in Jesus, He will give us the shield of faith, with which we *will be able to quench all the fiery darts of the wicked one* (Ephesians 6:16). When Zacharias, John the Baptist's father, prophesied about Jesus, he called Him the horn of salvation: *[God] has raised up a horn of salvation for us in the house of His servant David* (Luke 1:69). Christ is our stronghold that triumphs over enemy strongholds: *For the weapons of our warfare are not carnal but mighty in God for pulling down strongholds, casting down arguments and every high thing that exalts itself against the knowledge of God, bringing every thought into captivity to the obedience of Christ* (2 Corinthians 10:4–5). If you have yet to do so, call upon the Lord Jesus Christ for your salvation, for He is worthy to be praised. If you do so, He will save you from the great Enemy—Satan—as well as from eternal damnation. *Whoever calls on the name of Lord shall be saved* (Joel 2:32; Acts 2:21; Romans 10:13).

V. Discussion Questions

1. What stood out to you about this lesson and the passages discussed?

2. *I will love You, O Lord, my strength.* How will you love the Lord?

3. *The Lord is my rock and my fortress and my deliverer; my God, my strength, in whom I will trust.* How does the Lord's ability to protect you help you trust in Him?

4. *My shield and the horn of my salvation, my stronghold.* In what ways can the Lord help you combat spiritual warfare?

5. *I will call upon the Lord, who is worthy to be praised.* What are some reasons you praise the Lord?

6. *So shall I be saved from my enemies.* How has the Lord saved you from your enemies?

7. Is there anything that you can take away from this discussion and apply to your life? Any final thoughts?

www.ingramcontent.com/pod-product-compliance
Lightning Source LLC
Chambersburg PA
CBHW080839120626
46553CB00009B/2490